W0389790

My Time
with the
Master

My Time with the Master

Paramahamsa Prajnanananda

ISBN 3-902038-08-X

PUBLISHED BY
Prajna Publication, Diefenbachgasse 38/6, 1150 Vienna, Austria, Europe

PRINTED AT
Ueberreuter Print und Digimedia, 2100 Korneuburg/Austria

DEDICATION

A Medieval poet and saint from India, Ravidas, wrote the following poem which describes the relationship between God and his devotee. This beautiful poem makes me think of Gurudev.

You are sandalwood. I am water.
(The sandalwood gives the water fragrance.)
You are a black cloud. I am a peacock.
(The peacock's heart dances with the sight of the black cloud.)
You are the pearl and I am the thread.
(I have no value, but in union with you I gain my purpose.)
You arc my Father and Mother, and I am the child.
(I have grown through your care and love.)
You are my friend. I am your companion.
(We are held together in divine friendship.)
You are the river and I am a small tributary.
(I have merged in you to be united in the ocean of divine consciousness.)
You are the tree, and I am the fruit and flower.
(Whatever I am it is because of you.)
You are my everything, in reality nothing belongs to me.
On this special day, I dedicate my heartfelt love and complete devotion to you.

Humbly
Prajnanananda

27th of May, 2001

ACKNOWLEDGEMENT

My eternal gratitude to my Guruji, who has been the source of inspiration and guidance throughout my life. My special love to Harinath and Suddha Bathina, and to Prathima and Hassan Srinidhi for their love in compiling this book, to Irma Botero for her dedication in proofreading and editing this work, to Martin Gostentschnig and Traude Wukits for the many hours they spent transcribing various manuscripts into the present shape, to Ulla Graf for choosing the pictures and typing the selected correspondence, to Anneliese Mixan for her timely help in everything that was needed, to Georg Wachberger for his creative ideas in designing the cover and layout and to Alessandra Weber for thorough proofreading and taking the responsibility for the production process.

God will bless them.

With Love,

Prajnanananda

CONTENTS

SECTION I

- Flow of Time -

CHAPTER THREE

The Passage of Time

CHAPTER FOUR

Drawing Me to the West

CHAPTER FIVE

My New Life

CHAPTER SIX

Divinity Manifested Through Renunciation

SECTION II

- Reflections of my Master's Mind -

ILLUSTRATIONS

SELECTED LETTERS

1. The soul-stirring first letter, 1986
2. Transmitting his care and love
3. You are in my daily thoughts
4. His encouragement, 1988
5. Your letter gives divinity, 1986
6. Practical instructions
7. Scriptural discussion
8. His assurance
9. His trust
10. God is at your hand
11. His concern
12. Signs of the Guru
13. His greetings
14. His wishes

SECTION I

- Flow of Time -

Recollections

Prologue

Every individual needs to grow in every aspect of life. Physical and intellectual growth are essential requirements but without spiritual growth, the real beauty of a person remains unmanifested.

Skills and talents are developed through the love and care of our parents, the sincerity of our teachers and the discipline acquired in schools and Universities.

To cultivate timeless spiritual values like love, calmness and peace, to learn to live without stress, in a balanced way, inspite of the turmoils of life, we need to build a strong spiritual foundation.

For spiritual growth and the manifestation of our divine qualities, we need a teacher, a guide, a Guru, a preceptor or a Master, who through his exemplary behavior, strong spiritual foundation, deep scriptural knowledge and realization, can mould and shape the life of the student and open the way to the path of self-realization.

Every sincere seeker, with the help of a spiritual guide, tries to eradicate stumbling stones like ego, jealousy and hatred, and transforms his/her life and fills it with love, purity and devotion.

Once the chosen Guru is found, a sincere student will blossom under his care. A Guru, in the Holy Scriptures is described as the mystical philosopher's stone that is able to turn ordinary metal into gold. But a Guru's power goes beyond that, he can transform ordinary metal into another philosopher's stone. A true teacher knows through divine insight, the mind and thought pattern of his disciples. With these tools, he guides them to achieve their true potential.

In these pages lie some fragments of my life with my Master. Personal experiences are hard to portray in a written form. Life's picture is far too complex to be depicted in black and white. But this story needed to be told, not only as a tribute to my divine Master but also as a source of inspiration to all travelers in search of truth.

The Guru-disciple relationship is not easy. Many sacrifices are needed in order to grow in the spiritual path. Meeting my Master was the turning point in my life. For more than twenty years of close association, I have struggled to serve my Master who represents for me the essence of spirituality.

In return, my Guru has given me the biggest blessing of all, he has helped to accelerate my spiritual evolution. Our bond is complete; he is my father, I am his child, we walk together as father and son. I have grown through his love and wisdom.

CHAPTER ONE

The Discovery

Only through God's grace may we obtain those three rarest advantages – human birth, the longing for liberation, and discipleship to an illumined teacher.

Viveka Choodamani of Sri Shankaracharya

When I travel from place to place, meeting new people and new students, many of them ask how I met Gurudev for the first time. In human life, especially in spiritual life, the role of the teacher, the role of the spiritual Master is vital. Through the love of the Guru, the spiritual guide, one gets inner transformation and spiritual evolution. When one finds the right spiritual guide in life, the major task of self-transformation is accelerated.

A Distant Echo in my Mind

As I recollect my first physical encounter with Gurudev, I remember how I first heard about him. I was about fourteen years of age when I saw an article in the local Oriya newspaper about him. In that newspaper there was news of Shri Gurudev's first return from the West and a detailed explanation of his successful trip to many European countries. At that time I only knew about Swami Vivekananda, the disciple of Shri Ramakrishna, who was the first Indian monk to go abroad to America and some European countries in 1893, to spread the spiritual wisdom of India. So I was surprised to know about another monk in the seventies (1974-75), teaching about India's spiritual tradition of Yoga in the West. I was thrilled to know that he was not far from my native place. He was in Puri, Orissa. This was the first time, but I forgot about this. Later on I read two or three articles of Gurudev, in the newspaper, related to the significance of religious festivals like Durga Puja, and Saraswati Puja and idol worship. At that time I did not know who he was, but his name had a strong impact on my mind, as if I knew him from somewhere.

My First Impression of Puri

My second experience was in the later part of 1974, when I visited Puri for the first time, with other students from my school. We were going from the seashore towards the Jagannath Temple. On the way I stopped suddenly looking at a small narrow road. At the entrance was a wooden sign with the letters "Karar Ashram, Kriya Yoga Meditation Center, founded by Swami Shriyukteshwarji", written in color and very small in size. When I read this, I felt like I knew this road and I knew this name. Again I joined my friends and as I came towards the Jagannath Temple, I do not know why I had the strange feeling that I knew all these roads, especially the way to the Karar Ashram. But what was this Karar Ashram?

I did not understand why this was happening to me. In the Indian spiritual tradition, it is believed that the Guru-disciple relationship is eternal, it is not limited to this life and it is also believed that until the disciple is completely realized, the Guru comes in some form or other to guide the student. Paramahamsa Yogananda himself promised, "I will come again and again to evolve you all in the spiritual path and to lead you to the goal of realization." It might be that I had a predestined Guru, not only the relationship of this lifetime, but of previous births.

The third experience was actually seeing Gurudev's picture. I was studying in Ravenshaw College, Cuttack, living in a hostel. When I visited my friend Arun Chatterjee's room I saw hanging on the wall in a small glass frame, pictures of five Gurus, Babaji, Lahiri Mahasaya, Shriyukteshwar, Yogananda and in the middle was a small passport size photo in black and white of Gurudev Baba Hariharananda. When I looked at these photos I was almost in a state of trance. I knew all these faces in all these photos, but who were they? I told my friend that I knew all these monks. He was amazed, "You know them? Are you initiated? Can you please tell me who they are?" While I was looking at the photo of Gurudev I replied, " I do not know their names but I do know all of them. They are all familiar to me." My friend, his parents, and all his family were already initiated into Kriya Yoga. He told the names of the Masters, pointing out the pictures to me. Looking at the pictures made a strong impression in me. It may have been the previous knowledge of another birth, but their memory was strongly imprinted in my brain.

The Strong Desire Within Me

Life passes through many transitions and transformations. It was such a period in my life from my late teens up to my twenties. I had the clear vision of my life and the path to travel, but I did not have a true guide, a Guru. During this time, I was constantly praying to God to guide me through a spiritual Master. Whenever any monk visited my hometown or Cuttack, where I did most of my studies, I made a special trip to see him and spend time with him. By God's grace, many spiritual Masters were passing through every month and there was no lack of spiritual activities. I had the good fortune and opportunity to have the rare company of many holy saints, monks, and spiritual teachers and to listen to their elevated teachings from early childhood. Yet, insistently I prayed inwardly to God, "Oh God, show me the way, give me a Guru who can really lead me to reach the spiritual goal of life." During that time there was a big *yajna,* a fire ceremony conducted under the auspices of the *Shankaracharya* of Kanchi Kamakoti Peetham. It was a really big *yajna.* Qualified priests from South India, following strict Vedic discipline, were conducting the ceremony on the banks of the river *Mahanadi.* I kept going there every day, and spent many hours looking at the fire, inwardly meditating and praying to God. On the last day of this fire ceremony, during its completion, *purnahuti,* a last oblation was given to the blazing fire accompanied with holy Vedic *mantras*. The priests announced that if anybody had a wish to be fulfilled, if they prayed to God sincerely during that time, surely their wish would come true. I was sitting there looking at the blazing fire rising higher and higher with the *ghee*, clarified butter, poured into the fire continuously for more than one hour with chanting of a long Vedic *mantra*. I was praying to God for nothing except to grant me self-realization with the help of a Guru, a guide. This was my one and only prayer. After praying with such single-minded concentration, the real physical encounter came.

The Extraordinary Monk

The same year, one winter evening, I saw in the newspaper that Swami Hariharananda Giri, the world famous Kriya Yogi was in town, residing in the house of one of his disciples, Dr. Niranjan Pradhan, and anyone interested could come and have his *darshan* and *satsang*. The moment I saw this news, a great thrill reverberated in my heart. This was meant for me. I immediately set out to go to this Doctor's house. After a long walk, asking people for directions on the way, I finally reached my destination. It was evening time and getting dark earlier than usual because of winter. I entered a big villa, surrounded by a beautiful garden full of flowers and fruits. It was a beautiful, well-furnished house. In the huge living room, there was a bed on which a monk was seated very nicely dressed in ochre color. Many people were already sitting in that room, as I slowly entered. In India, it is a tradition that when a person enters into the presence of a monk, one should kneel down and bow. I knelt down from a distance and bowed down to him and he responded with his folded hands. I did not dare to go near and touch his feet because many traditional monks do not allow anyone to touch their feet. I silently sat in a corner, my eyes following every movement and my ears listening to every word. As he sat there he looked like a beautiful rose in full bloom, yet many springs had passed since he was already seventy-three years old. His inner beauty transfixed me. It was not only his appearance, it was the sweetness in his voice, the polite way he would treat others and above all, the gracefulness of his gestures. At the same time that I was so full of admiration, I also felt some confusion. His clothes looked too expensive as did his gold-rimmed glasses; his hair was shampooed and well groomed. From childhood, my idea of monasticism was a life of complete renunciation, asceticism and detachment with no material comforts. A very simple lifestyle and very simple clothing. When I saw how different he looked to the many monks that had crossed my path I was disconcerted. To add to my bewilderment was a discussion on vegetarianism. I was a complete vegetarian, not even taking onion or garlic. I was sitting in the corner of the room listening with great interest to the views of a realized monk on vegetarianism. A disciple was strongly advocating vegetarianism and fervently condemning foods such as fish and meat. In the course of this conversation Swami Hariharananda asked him, "Why do you take so much fish and meat?" This man was taken aback and argued, "I am a vegetarian, I don't take fish or meat." So Baba answered, "Look, when you speak so much about fish and animal flesh, how bad they are, you are constantly thinking about those things. If your mind is always thinking about these things even in a negative way, you are mentally trying to enjoy those things. So do not eat mentally. Physical eating through the mouth is not the only kind of eating. If one eats through the mind it is also eating." At first I could not understand this subtle train of thought. My whole traditional upbringing rebelled inside. An Indian monk should encourage people to be purely vegetarian. Why did this unusual monk talk like that? But Baba Hariharananda pressed his point, "Don't think that only by taking vegetarian food one will realize God. If this were true, then all the cows, goats and the deer in the forest would all be God-realized. Don't think that by going to holy places and taking a bath in the waters of the holy rivers like the *Ganga* or the *Yamuna*, one will be God-realized. Then all the fish and aquatic creatures in the water of holy rivers would be God-realized. If only by eating fruits one will get realization, then all the monkeys living on the trees that live on fruits are God-realized." He proceeded to sing a song of Meera, which contained the above-mentioned message. He finished by urging all of us not to spend time and energy discussing and debating about food, but to spend our time on God. I was amazed and confused yet his unusual approach made an impact on my mind. I was forced to modify my previous concepts.

I Bowed Down for the First Time

It was getting late in the evening and towards nine o'clock the devotees and disciples were bowing down to him and taking their leave. When I saw all of them touching his feet, I did not want to miss the opportunity to touch the feet of this holy person. Many people ask, "Why do people touch the feet of monks, sages or holy saints?" They cannot easily comprehend, especially those who are born in the West and grown up in a Western culture, submerged in the values of a different civilization. When Westerners meet, they greet each other by shaking hands and hugging each other. Kneeling down, bowing down and touching the feet is new to them. And yet in the holy books like the Bible, the Bhagavad Gita and other scriptures like the Upanishads or the Koran, the tradition of bowing down exists. In the Bible, in several places in the Old Testament, there is a clear description of one lying flat on the ground and bowing to an elder or an honorable person. In the New Testament there is the description of kneeling down and kissing the feet of the teacher, kissing the feet of Jesus.

In the Bhagavad Gita it is said,

tadviddhi pranipātena pariprasnena
sevayā upadakṣanti te jñānam jñāniinaḥ
tattvadarśinaḥ

'When you go to the realized Masters, Men of Wisdom, prostrate yourself to them, ask proper questions with humility, serve them, and they will teach you and give you knowledge.'

The Gita - IV.34

What is the purpose? Why should one bow down? When one kneels, keeping the head down and performing a bow, it is a good yogic exercise. It has lots of impact on the body and the mind. When one bows down, the ego also comes down. One bows down to a person who is senior in age, or more experienced in knowledge, or more advanced in spiritual wisdom, as a mark of respect. A bow also expresses an attitude of surrender to a teacher, a sign that you are ready to learn from him. The human body has two poles; one pole is in the fontanel and the other pole is in the feet. When one bows down and touches the feet of the Master with the forehead, the North Pole is touching the South Pole, or feet. This completes the circuit; North and South poles are joined together. The spiritual energy of a highly advanced person will cross to the body of the person who is bowing down to him/her. In a simple gesture one gains spiritual energy, and at the same time one loses a certain amount of negative propensities while becoming charged with spirituality.

When I first bowed to the Master, touching his feet, I remained on my knees and with folded hands looked up at his beautiful smile. He started talking to me. This was the first conversation between Baba and me. He asked me, "Are you a student?" I replied, "Yes." "What do you study?" I said, "Economics." "Very good. You must be living in a hostel." I was surprised, how could he know that I lived in a hostel? He talked with me for at least fifteen minutes explaining how I should live in a hostel without coming under the influence of bad habits. I was really happy to have met such a rare monk. Prior to that I have seen many monks from my childhood, the monks who lived in the nearby *mathas,* or monasteries, in my native place, many wandering monks and many monks in holy places like Puri. Those monks all had their distinctive merit, but were completely different from the one to whom I was talking. Gurudev was unusual in more ways than one. Strangely, I felt close to him and he was talking as if he knew me and cared for me. He wanted me to be free, to be pure and to lead a life of discipline. This happened to be my most cherished desire. As I bowed down again, he tried to hold my hair, but failed since my hair was very short. So in a fatherly gesture he moved his hand over my head in a gesture full of love. He patted me on my cheeks and chin with great affection. Towards the end, he said, "Come again. I am very happy to see you." A highly spiritual monk, who dwelled in such an elevated state of spiritual ecstasy, with an extremely busy schedule, touring and traveling all over the world was talking to a twenty-year old. His words penetrated my heart and I was thinking, "Who is he? Why does he love me so much? Why does he talk like this? Does he really love me?" During that whole night I could not sleep. I was recollecting what he said over and over, how he looked and how he was so sweet and humble. His talk had fascinated me to such a strong degree, that it made a lasting impression on my mind.

The Second Visit

The next day I couldn't resist the temptation of visiting him again. So I followed the same path as before. When I approached him and bowed down, touching his feet, he said, "You have come again. I am so happy. Please sit down." At that time there were very few people. Slowly more and more people came until the room was filled with disciples. That day there were no new initiations. I was the only one there who was not initiated. As a tradition during Kriya meditation, those not initiated into Kriya are not allowed to sit in the guided meditation session. So before starting meditation, Baba asked, "Is there anybody who is not initiated? If so, please leave the room for some time till the meditation is finished. After the meditation is over, you can come inside again and sit here." I stood up to leave with due humility and honor Gurudev's word. But he said, "You please sit down here, you need not go." I sat down with eyes closed and listened to Baba while he guided the meditation class. I did not practice, as Baba was guiding Kriya meditation, but I enjoyed entering into a deeper state of meditation, while listening to his instructions with the utmost attentiveness and seriousness.

That day there was another coincidence. One of my friends, Sujogya, a student of English Literature, who stayed in the same hostel as I did, was also there. He was an initiated disciple of Gurudev. When he saw me, he was really very happy and elated to find me there. By God's grace, I was academically a very well accomplished student and this gave me a certain popularity within the student community. At the end of meditation, I went once again to bow down to Gurudev. He showered me with many blessings and invited me to come again and not to forget him. But the next day, Baba left the neighborhood and went to other towns in Orissa. I had no further opportunity to see him for a while.

Many links, however, had been re-established. When I came back to the hostel, my friend came to my room and started talking about the greatness of Gurudev and his love and spiritual power. I heard all these things and I was really happy to know such a great Soul, a living, realized Master, full of love and affection, even for a person like me. But I was not yet convinced that he was the Guru I was looking for. Up to that point I had seen many spiritual Masters and reputed monks in contemporary Indian spiritual communities. Many venerable monks had asked me to come and get initiation from them. I had even made a specific trip to the Himalayas. All this while, I remained uncertain of how to recognize my spiritual guide. Among all the monks I met throughout my life, Baba Hariharanandaji was the one who touched my heart and soul and who overpowered me with his compassion, love and kindness. But still, at that time, I did not know for sure if he was my Guru or not.

I remembered in this context a saying of Shri Ramakrishna Paramahamsa, a great saint, mystic and divine Master of the 19th Century, "When you get some money from a stranger, you check it carefully to see whether it is genuine or fake. When you go to a spiritual person to accept him as your guide, be careful in judging him. Look at him during the day and during the night." During the daytime, a person may seem fascinating through his talk or behavior, at night the same thing may not be true. It is advisable to know a person completely and thoroughly, before you accept him/her as your spiritual guide. From my childhood and adolescence I had read much about the teachings of Shri Ramakrishna, his instruction on how to choose a Guru had a strong influence on me. For sometime I considered joining the monastic order of the Ramakrishna Mission. I also vividly remembered the teaching of Jesus, in the Gospel of Mathew, which stated that there were many false prophets, posing as spiritual teachers, like wolves hiding in sheep's clothing. I constantly prayed to God and asked him, "Oh God, who is my real Guru, how will I know him?"

Another Sign

During this period, another thing happened which greatly influenced my life. Near my college, there was a bookshop from where I regularly borrowed books to read. Fortunately, I was in the best terms with most of the booksellers in Cuttack, they would let me borrow whichever book I wanted to read, even brand new books, and I would handle every book with extreme care, not damaging the pages and would return them intact. This was a great privilege, as a student's budget does not stretch such a long way as to allow one to buy all the books one would like to read. A few weeks after meeting Gurudev, my eyes were drawn to a particular book on a shelf. It was 'Autobiography of a Yogi' by Paramahamsa

Yogananda. It was really a fascinating book and I was attracted to the path of Kriya in a very subtle way. At that time I was leading a strict disciplined life. From morning to night, I spent most of my free time reading holy books, trying to meditate, doing some chanting, visiting temples or monks and sages and participating in social work to help people in need. I tried not to waste a single minute. I even observed silence for a certain period of time daily and had already thorough control over my food habits and practiced regularly certain yogic postures. I was not so disciplined in attending my classes at the University, since I was not very interested in them. A humorous incident happened one day as I was reading 'Autobiography of a Yogi'. I fell asleep with the open book on my chest. A friend of mine came into my room and looking at the picture of Yogananda from a distance, remarked, "Oh! You pose yourself to be a monk, to be a Baba, but you keep the photo of the Mona Lisa on your chest while you are sleeping nicely." I woke up at the sound of his voice and exclaimed, "Where is the Mona Lisa? Come and have a closer look and see who he is." When he read the name, Paramahamsa Yogananda, he was really surprised as well as ashamed of the hastiness of his remark. He was also full of curiosity and asked me if he was a monk. I said, "Yes, a monk from India who spent most of his life in the United States, teaching spiritual life, Yoga and meditation to people in the West. He is a true messenger of India's spiritual tradition." Even now when I look at Paramahamsa Yoganandaji, I think how he really became the Mona Lisa of my life. I love him. I love him much more than anyone else, with the same devotion and love I have reserved for my own Guru.

The Karar Ashram

Soon after this, I heard about the celebration of the 'Foundation Day' of the Karar Ashram in Puri, which falls on March 22nd, the day of the vernal equinox. It was the very same Ashram that had strangely drawn me as a teenager. Swami Shriyukteshwarji, the Guru of Paramahamsa

Yogananda and Baba Hariharananda, founded the Karar Ashram in 1903. The significance of the vernal equinox is that both day and night are of equal duration. This is a special day for all Yogis to meditate, contemplate and quicken their spiritual evolution. Every year Baba Hariharanandaji was present during this festival. As soon as I knew about this special celebration, I wanted to go to the Karar Ashram. When I consulted my friend Sujogya, who was already a Kriyavan, he explained that only initiated disciples could go there because several guided meditations would take place. I was insistent, "I might not be allowed to take part in the meditation, but I would still like to go and see other Kriyavans, the Ashram, and above all Gurudev." He was still reluctant to take me. Only with the utmost persuasion could I change his mind, "If you take me to the Ashram I will pay your travel expenses. Let us go together and I will manage all other matters there." Finally he accepted and we found ourselves on our way to Puri.

The Samadhi Temple

This was the first time in this life, that I visited the Karar Ashram. We reached there around the 19th of March, a few days before the celebration of the 'Foundation Day', and stayed a few days afterwards. The Ashram was overcrowded with disciples, not only from all over India but also from the West. There was no place to rest, but at night we managed to sleep in the porch of Shriyukteshwar's *Samadhi Mandir*. It is a beautiful place, full of serenity, extreme calmness and strong spiritual vibrations. During the day I tried to get closer to Baba, to sit near him and listen to him. Just a glimpse of him filled my heart with joy. He always remained loving and compassionate, and his presence was very elevating. I began to forget all worldly things, and my mind roamed in high levels of spiritual ecstasy. Other times, when Baba was not available, I just sat in the Temple of Shriyukteshwar, looking at the marble statue of this great Guru, in his *Samadhi Mandir*. *Samadhi Mandir* means 'where the body is buried'. The body of a monk is usually not cremated. It is either buried under the ground, in a sitting meditative position called *bhoo-samadhi,* or submerged in the deep flow of the river or the ocean with a ritual called *jalasamadhi.* The *Samadhi Mandir,* in the premises of the Karar Ashram in Puri, is one of the most beautiful places I have ever visited in my life. A place of real meditation, where the mind is easily drawn into inner spiritual experience. Although there were initiations taking place, I was not inwardly ready to take initiation. I kept observing Baba day and night, following the counsel of Shri Ramakrishna, I sat near him in his bedroom, in the meditation room and also walked with him in the garden carrying his cushion. Everybody thought that I was his disciple, and I felt inner contentment.

Foundation Day Celebration

During this time, disciples and devotees from all over the world, gathered in this holy Ashram. The small premises were slowly crowded. There was hardly any room in the meditation hall.

The most memorable day was the 22nd of March. On this day of balance and equanimity, Yogis feel a special union with God and his creation.

The sunrise and the sunset were at a quarter to six. At this auspicious time, all the disciples gathered, awaiting the presence of Gurudev. The conch blew, it broke the silence of nature evoking a deep spiritual vibration. All proceeded towards the Temple of Shriyukteswar. There was meditation, chanting of prayers and devotional songs, even holy *arati*, little lamps that were lit to honor the divine Guru, Shriyukteswarji. Baba conducted all the activities.

After this initial ceremony, we made our way to the meditation hall. Everyone took a seat. Baba came in and sat on the *dais,* accompanied by other monks and *yogacharyas.* I had the chance to see Gurudev's elder brother Dr. S.N. Bhattacharya, a medical doctor and his family. He came with his wife and two grand daughters. The melody of the devotional songs thrilled everyone's heart. The disciples stood in line, and one after the other touched the feet of Gurudev and got his blessings.

This day is indelible in my memory. Every disciple came with flowers or a flower garland, some offered a donation and fruits. Some devotees were so moved by their inner experience that you could see tears in their eyes.

The entire day was full of festivities. At a quarter to six, there was a special service in the Temple, followed by *satsang sabha*. A few advanced Kriya Yogis spoke on diverse spiritual topics and the intricacies of Kriya Yoga. Everyone waited expectantly for Gurudev's talk to culminate this great event. This was the first time that I heard him speak in front of such a vast audience, in many languages simultaneously.

Although his body was looking tired due to the excessive strain, his love and energy overflowed in every word, in every gesture. I could clearly see the glory of the Guru, an inspired glow giving a special light to his countenance. All the visitors were given a good meal and Baba retired to his room almost at midnight.

It is a longstanding tradition, from the time of Shriyukteshwarji, that on the 23rd of March, in the afternoon, all devotees along with their spiritual guide go to the Temple of Jagannath. As the heir of Shriyukteshwarji, Gurudev followed faithfully this sacred custom every year.

Hundreds of devotees and disciples followed Shri Gurudev on the streets of Puri, singing devotional songs. It was a grand spectacle. Jagannath Temple is thousands of years old and a place of worship of Lord Jagannath, the Lord of the Universe. People from all over the world come to see this Temple. Spiritual seekers of all paths pay homage to Lord Jagannath.

When Gurudev came back from the Temple, his blood pressure was extremely low and he had to stay in bed. A doctor and another disciple were inside the room, monitoring his blood pressure and taking good care of him. Although nobody was allowed, I managed to go inside and sit near him, touching his feet. Looking at his calm and quiet body lying on the bed, I thought of how hard he worked for his disciples, and took so much strain on his own body. That evening I prayed, "Oh God, I get so much love, so much compassion, so much inner peace and purity in the company of this monk. If he is my Guru please convince me inwardly."

The Dream

Next month, in April, a strange thing happened. I had continued my prayers and meditation as usual. Close to dawn, on a Wednesday, I had a dream and this dream changed my life. I dreamt of Gurudev (this was my first dream of him), in a new place, which I had not seen before. It was not the Puri Ashram, but I remember a meditation hall with a beautiful garden around it. In the meditation hall there were eight to ten people and Baba was initiating me. Until that time my idea of initiation was of a Guru uttering a *mantra* in the ear of the disciple. I hailed from a Brahmin *kulaguru* family. My father himself is the *kulaguru* of many families and he initiated people in this way. So to me 'initiation' meant getting a *mantra* from the Guru and using that *mantra* for chanting or meditation. But in this dream the initiation was really different. In this initiation, he was touching my whole spine and different *chakras* and it brought a thrilling sensation in me with beautiful inner experience. It felt very real even though it was just a dream. I woke up wondering what the dream meant. I rationalized it was only a dream; it could have been because I was thinking of Baba all the time and hoping for a clear sign of who was to be my Guru. These recurrent thoughts had combined to create this particular dream. I spent the day in a very joyful state of inner peace and calmness, but I gave no further importance to the dream. This is the play of mind, which is not easily convinced. The next night, around the same time, I experienced the same dream; before my eyes the same place appeared with the same hall, the same people sitting around and Baba was once again initiating me. It was an exact repetition of the previous initiation. I woke up and thought, "Why do I see the same dream again and again?" My rationalistic mind stopped analyzing and I decided to approach Baba and ask him directly if he was my Guru and if he would accept me as his disciple. I had already read in many holy books, that the Guru-disciple relationship is predestined. So if I were predestined to be his disciple he would accept me.

Journey to Puri

That Thursday morning, I immediately made my way to Puri with two of my friends, Indrabhushan and Shaktibrata, who studied in the same college. They wanted to go to Puri to visit Lord Jagannath and also to see the Ashram. I went to the Karar Ashram first, to find out the whereabouts of Baba and to my great surprise he was still there. Usually at the end of March he leaves for the West. It was around noontime. Baba had finished his lunch and was resting. The door of his room was almost closed. I entered into the Ashram premises and first of all went to Shriyukteshwar's Temple. Surrendering myself, I bowed down, and paid homage to this great Yogi with a heartfelt prayer. Then, I came towards the residential part of the Ashram and I sat waiting, under the shade of a big *bilwa* tree, known as wood-apple. It is considered to be a very holy tree. The leaves are used for worship in the temples of Shiva, Kali and Durga. The fruit is edible, nutritious and healthy. The bark as well as the leaves are used in ayurvedic medicine. Even the wood is used for special rituals in Hinduism. The *brahmacharis* knew me from my previous visits to the Ashram. One of them approached me and inquired about the purpose of my visit. I expressed my wish to see Gurudev and talk to him privately. He explained that it was the day in which Gurudev observed silence and if I would wait till the evening meditation was over, then surely I would have the opportunity to talk with him. I was a little disappointed as I was not prepared to stay so long in Puri and if I had to wait till the evening I could not go back to Cuttack that same day. I had not come alone. Not sure about what to do, I just sat there and prayed to God. After a while, another *brahmachari* came and asked me if he could help me. When he heard my request, he went to Baba's room and after some time came out and told me I could go inside. Gurudev was relaxing on his bed. Nobody was there. I entered and he silently indicated to me to bolt the door from the inside. Then to my great surprise he broke his silence. I bowed down to him and he asked me," Baba, (in this case it was lovingly meant as little father) what happened, what do you want?" I said, "Baba, you know what I want." He replied, "Yes, I know. Tell me in your own words what you need." I expressed my desire to be initiated and asked, "Am I ready to be initiated?" Then he said, "You are already initiated. What more do you need?" I said, "How? I want to be initiated directly by you." Then Baba became very happy and he said, "I know that you were a little hesitant about being initiated as you wanted to know for certain who your real guide was. Secondly, you were afraid that if I initiated you, other monks who love you might not love you, in future. But remember, once I initiate you, everybody will love you. Once the indelible stamp of Hariharananda is imprinted on your heart, no one can ever erase it. You will get all-round development and realization." I was relieved to hear this assurance from Gurudev. Then he said, "I will not initiate you now. Next Thursday you will come to the Bhubaneshwar Ashram. I will initiate you there. Can you come and stay with me for one week?" I assured him I could. "Will it not hamper your education, your regular classes at college?" he asked. I told him, "No." Then he instructed me, "You come with a mosquito net. You will stay for seven days with me, you will meditate with me and you will learn meditation nicely." My joy knew no bounds. I bowed down to Baba, filled with great happiness as I had finally found my Guru. My heart and mind were overflowing with love and gratitude due to the rarest achievement of life, to be affirmed by the Guru. I requested to Baba to allow my two friends to have his *darshan* and then we left.

In God's creation, if you want something and sincerely pray to God for that purpose, God answers your prayer. No sincere prayer remains unfulfilled. God had answered my prayer. It was now clear who my Guru and guide was. But I had to wait another week to get initiation. With my two friends I went to thank the Lord in the Jagannath Temple, and that same evening we returned to Cuttack. Once there, another friend, Manoranjan, after learning of my plans and even though he knew nothing about Gurudev or Kriya Yoga, expressed his desire to be also initiated and to come with me. The week seemed to be very long. Since neither one of us knew where the Ashram in Bhubaneshwar was located we collected information from different sources. When we started on our journey, it turned out that we were given the wrong directions to the Ashram.

The Dream Comes True

We got down at the wrong railway station and found that there was no connecting train again till evening. So we walked and walked, quite a few miles, on that hot summer afternoon, under the scorching sun and finally found the Ashram. As we opened the door and went inside, I was really amazed that it was the place of my dream with the same garden, and the same meditation hall! There was a monk living there whom I had already seen in the Karar Ashram Foundation Day Celebration. After saluting him in the traditional way, I told him about my appointment with Gurudev for next day's initiation and my intention to stay there for one week. He showed us a place to store our luggage and made us comfortable.

It was almost evening. Many disciples, nearly twenty to thirty, were waiting for Baba to come from Puri to Bhubaneshwar. It was getting dark, when a car finally entered the Ashram grounds with Gurudev sitting in the back. When he got down from the car, all the devotees surrounded him and started bowing down to him. I was standing in the background, listening to him talking with the monk in charge. His very first words to this monk were about me. Baba said, "Two college students will come from Cuttack and they will be initiated tomorrow. One of them will stay longer in order to meditate with me." As I listened, I was really surprised about two things; first of all that such a great Yogi, so busy, would remember me. Secondly, that he could foresee that two of us were coming. A week ago we had only talked about one initiation. Once again I was struck about how easily Gurudev could anticipate my thoughts and my movements. The monk in charge made all the arrangements for our accommodation and food.

The next morning was the initiation. On the day of my initiation I wore a white *dhoti* in the traditional Indian style. I was sitting among six or seven people to be initiated and there were also some older disciples. My attention and thought was constantly focused on God. Gurudev and the other monk were initiating the new students, by turns. When it was my turn the other monk called me, "Come to me for initiation." I was really shocked. How could I refuse? But I wanted to be initiated by Shri Gurudev. To my great relief, Gurudev interrupted and said, "No. Please come to me." Looking at the other Swami, he explained gently, "He will come to me." I went towards Shri Gurudev, bowed down at his feet and he started the ceremony. The initiation was a mirror of my previous dream. I felt the same joy, the same thrill. What was somewhat unusual was that Gurudev made some remarks about my life, specially regarding my future, which subsequently came true. My spine, brain, mind and heart were charged with love, as I experienced keenly the triple divine qualities.

When initiation was finished, everyone left the hall but I continued sitting alone, listening to the beautiful divine sound since I was not sure where it was coming from. After a while I started searching everywhere to find out the cause of the sound, but there was no trace of any machine, so I came out. Outside I could also hear the sound. Then I realized it was within me. I was surprised how on the day of initiation, I could listen so clearly to this sound. I went to Gurudev's room and as though he knew my doubt, he asked me, "Do you hear the sound?" I replied, "Yes, Baba. I am hearing the sound continuously without closing the ears." Baba smiled contentedly and added, "You are fortunate to hear the sound continuously on the day of your initiation. I bless you. You'll surely progress rapidly in your spiritual life."

The Auspicious Vision

On the same day another memorable and significant incident took place. From my childhood the writings and lives of some Indian spiritual Masters had had a strong impact on my life. I had the deepest love and respect for Shri Ramakrishna Paramahamsa, Swami Sivananda of the Divine Life Society in Rishikesh, Swami Nigamananda and Swami Swarupananda Paramahamsa. Swami Nigamananda is not so well known in West, but he was a great Yogi and a spiritual leader in the Eastern part of India. He lived a good period of time in Puri and left his body in the 1940's. I often visited his Ashram, which was close to my parents' house, near the place where I was born. I have read a couple of fascinating books written by this Yogi monk of high spiritual status. I had such a deep regard and veneration for him, that mentally I had always prayed for a Guru like him, to guide me in the spiritual path.

On the day of my initiation, at noontime, Baba was having lunch with ten to twelve disciples. Gurudev was sitting on the floor. All were seated in a rectangle and as the meal was served, after a prayer, we started eating. Gurudev and I were sitting face to face, at a distance of five to six feet from each other. While I was eating, my attention was not on the food. My mind was full of joy as I looked at Gurudev. His hair was tied in a knot on top of his head, as is the custom among many Indian monks. He had his left hand on the floor and with the right hand he was eating food. To my great surprise, as I looked at him, I saw Swami Nigamananda in his place, sitting in front of me. One may say it was a hallucination, but I looked three times to make sure, and Nigamananda was quietly looking at me. At the end of this play, the orange clad figure finally smiled. Then I saw, it was Baba. It was my strong feeling, that Baba was making it clear to me that in him lived the same spirit of Ramakrishna and of Nigamananda. He was just a personification to teach me and guide me in my spiritual life. I stayed seven days with Shri Gurudev. Every morning and evening we would meditate. The rest of the time I sat in his room, listening to his spiritual instructions. Occasionally, I served him in the Ashram garden or the kitchen. He always quoted directly from the scriptures with exact references. This is how I began my instruction.

When Baba was about to leave from Bhubaneshwar to Cuttack, he stopped the car and getting out, took me aside and asked me in a whisper, "Do you have money to go from Bhubaneshwar to Cuttack?" I said, "Yes Baba, I have." Then he said, "I have a strong desire to bring you in this car with me, but this car is already full with my host and his family, so there is no place for you to come, but I will be waiting for you in Cuttack, only then I will hold evening meditation."

This incident left a strong impression on my heart and mind. Here was a Guru who cared for my spiritual progress and for my welfare. Baba Hariharananda is a loving and caring Guru who touches every aspect of life. Being a college student, I might be out of funds after initiation and a week's stay in the Ashram. Gurudev expressed his love and concern by saying he wanted to take me with him in the car. His special consideration was the beginning of a strong bond between us. He was interested in my welfare, in my all-round development and I in turn wanted to learn about his spiritual heritage and to serve him loyally.

In Cuttack, Gurudev stayed in the residence of Dr. Pradham, where I had my first physical encounter with him. He stayed there for one week. Everyday, morning and evening I visited him and meditated near him. That year, God gave me a nice opportunity to be with him for fifteen days at a stretch, just after my initiation. Under his loving guidance, I tried to meditate and to practice Kriya sincerely, going deeper and deeper into meditation.

This was the beginning of my spiritual journey and Gurudev was my guide, the Master I had prayed for. In Kriya Yoga I had found all the elements I needed for my spiritual evolution. From that time onwards whenever Shri Gurudev was in Cuttack, Puri or Bhubaneshwar, I did not miss a single opportunity to be near him, to listen to him and to meditate under his direct guidance. Gurudev, in my view, is a living encyclopedia of holy books and scriptures. He has a remarkable, amazing memory. Every time he quoted the scriptures, he quoted with direct and accurate references.

As often as I could, I sat near him with a notebook, writing his teachings down. Just by listening to him, any ego I had on this subject was given up. He was rather old at that time, yet even at the age of seventy his brainpower was still strong. He was a fine teacher, and much of what I have learnt I owe directly to him and to the Gurus that came before him.

CHAPTER TWO

Divine Apprenticeship

uttiṣṭata jāgrata prāpya varān nibodhata
kṣurasya dhārā niśitā duratyayā durgam pathas
tat kavayo vadanti.

"Arise, awake, and learn by approaching the realized ones. The wise ones describe the path to be as impassable as a razor's edge, which when sharpened, is difficult to tread on."

Katha Upanishad I.3.14

Spiritual life needs a continuous effort. This path is slippery and extremely difficult. Only with the company of the Guru and the practice of his instructions, can a seeker evolve.

Shri Lahiri Mahasaya said each student of Kriya should try to be with his teacher one month in a year and when this was not possible, a week or at least three days. Only your teacher can verify the techniques. But it is much more subtle than that. An evolved Master can point the way and although the climb is yours to make, without his clear guidance you would slip again and again.

An Open Door

As I started my life near Gurudev, many small occurrences helped me shed light on his divine personality. When I stayed with Gurudev in the Karar Ashram, every morning I would go up to his room and take care of his breakfast and other minor tasks. The rest of the time, I would sit in his room answering letters, reading the mail, or meditating and listening to the metaphorical interpretation of the scriptures. One day, I saw that Baba's room was locked from the inside. There were two entrances to this room, but both the doors were closed. I hesitated to knock on the door, so I just waited outside. After one hour when the door was opened I entered inside and I bowed down to Gurudev. Gurudev asked me, "Where were you? I was expecting you to come over an hour ago." I told him that the door was closed and that I had sat outside, meditating. At this point, Baba assured me, "You are a green card holder. You do not require any visa to enter into this room. Whenever you want, at any time, you are always welcome. If the door is closed, then you should knock on the door and say, 'I am Triloki', you will find that the door will be opened for you. Nobody can stop you from entering this room. You are not separate from me." This incident helped me to understand the greatness of Gurudev's compassion and how his door would always be open to his sincere disciples. I felt symbolically, that his door would always be open for me.

Another incident took place in 1984. I was working in the office of the Karar Ashram, while Gurudev was outside having his picture taken with some of his disciples. I came out when the photo session was about to culminate. I was a little wistful since for quite some time I had longed to have a photograph taken with Baba. Gurudev read my mind and although he was already on his way to his room, he stopped in his tracks, turned around and asked the photographer to take a photograph of both of us together. My joy knew no bounds. I have kept that photograph with me to this day. It has a special place since it is the first photograph with Baba.

At another point, Gurudev was asking about my study and about my meditation. Then slowly the topic changed and he asked about my parents, brothers and sisters. When he inquired, "Where is your home?" I told him about the place where I was born. I thought that he would not know the location of this small, remote place and wanted to give him the name of a bigger town near my native place. Then he saw it clearly in his mind's eye, "When you get down at the bus stop there is a government guest house. Opposite the guesthouse, a road goes towards the West. Does this road lead to your home?" You will be surprised to know that it is exactly the road that leads to the village where I was born. Gurudev, with his enlightened mind could project images he had not seen with his physical eyes.

The Answer to my Questions

But more than anything, it was his way of dispelling my doubts that really made me appreciate what a great Master he was. I had just completed my master's degree examination and during that time I was a little confused. I had a strong desire to be a monk but I never talked with Baba about this. I was staying in the Ashram with Gurudev. I had a few questions to ask him, which I noted down on a piece of paper. There were about fifteen questions. I could not ask him directly though I was alone with him many times. I never talked to him much, only when he asked me something I would give him a short answer, directly to the point. My intention was to put the paper full of questions under his pillow. After his dinner, I arranged his bed and fixed the mosquito net around it. Since Baba was in the room, I could not place this paper under his pillow. When he was ready to retire for the night, I bowed down at his feet, before leaving the room. For a second, I thought of placing the paper with my questions at his feet. But in the end I decided against it. I left the room with a heavy heart.

The next morning, at 5.30 a.m. there was meditation in Baba's room. Four or five of us were meditating, while Baba was lying down on his bed and guiding us. The meditation lasted for one hour. During this memorable meditation, I was surprised that he answered all my questions, one after the other. After meditation, each one of us bowed down to Gurudev before leaving the room. Usually, I bowed to him after everybody was done, so that I could stay in the room looking at him and listening to him a bit longer. When it was my turn, I bowed down to him and he got hold of my hair with love and patted me on the cheeks asking, "Have I answered all your questions? Is there anything more?" I was really taken aback at the way he knew all my questions and thoughts. Although I could not ask these questions verbally or through paper, in that early morning, Gurudev answered all my questions, and silently dispelled my doubts.

I finished my master's degree examinations in January, 1983. Then I left home, indicating to my parents that I was going to Puri to live with Gurudev. I stayed in Bhubaneshwar and Puri with Gurudev for nearly two months.

He Called Me Back

When Gurudev left for Europe, I did not want to stay in the Ashram without him, so I silently left for the Himalayas. This was my second visit. In this stay in the Himalayas during the summer of 1983, I spent time meditating in a very serene Ashram environment. I met many monks, who both helped and later on encouraged me to live there permanently like a *brahmachari* or a monk. But the thought of Gurudev kept coming back to me strongly. It was during this time, that I discarded my usual clothes and started wearing simple white clothes, the attire of a *brahmachari*. One night, I saw Baba in a dream and he said, "Come back. Why do you stay here? Once you have accepted me as your spiritual guide, do you think that if you stay in the Himalayas or the banks of the *Ganga* you will get realization? You need the Guru's help. I will help you. Come back." This was a message for me, so I came back.

The Return

I was thinking of what to do next. I did not want to be a financial burden on my parents. During this period my master's exam results were out and I had graduated with honors. One day, I was sitting on the banks of the river *Mahanadi*, when my friend, Manoranjan walked up to me and said, "Do you know that you have been selected by the Directorate of

Higher Education of the Government of Orissa to teach Economics?" I was amazed; how could I get a job without applying for it. This friend, who had been initiated with me on the same day, had applied for the job on my behalf, obtaining all the necessary documents and testimonials from my parents and the University, in my absence. Because of my good academic credentials, I was considered for the job. I got the job in the College of Rourkela in October 1983. I joined as a member of the staff in November.

That year, Gurudev had come to Rourkela and had stayed at the residence of the Principal of the Engineering School. I did not know about that. Later on, during my free time, I went to Puri to be with Gurudev. I did not tell him about my job, but another disciple told Baba that I had been appointed as a lecturer, teaching Economics. On hearing this, Baba had exclaimed, "Who told you this? He is not a lecturer, he is not an Economist. He has not gone to college. Do you see his clothes? He is like a simple villager! He is my student. He will stay here and he will be a teacher of meditation." At that time I could not understand why Baba said this. I was a new student, practicing meditation just a little. I did not know much about meditation, in reality, I was teaching Economics. But I see now how his words came true. I am no longer a teacher of Economics. I am a student of Gurudev and I am trying to teach what he is teaching. Thereafter, while I worked as a lecturer at Rourkela and later on at Cuttack, I would try to be with Gurudev, during the holidays, wherever he was.

Doctor of Meditation

I will relate another incident. One day, while I was in Gurudev's room, an old disciple of Baba, who was also a Professor of Economics and knew me well, came into the room. Her name was Bijayalakshmi Ma, and she had been a disciple of Gurudev from her childhood. She came and hugged me in the presence of Baba. Hugging was not a common way to greet, so I felt a little shy. Then she added, "Do you know Baba, that Triloki

Baba is a good, brilliant student as well as an exceptional teacher. Please tell him that he can do some research work in Economics. He can contribute a lot in the field of Economics, for both students and society. Please tell him to take up research work for his doctorate." But Baba replied, "Do you know he has already got a doctorate?" I was as surprised as she was, we both looked at Baba curiously. Then Gurudev said, "He has a D.M. degree." She asked him what a D.M. degree meant. "It is Doctorate in Meditation. He has a degree in Meditation. He doesn't require any Ph.D. from any University." Many years passed. The human mind does not immediately grasp the teaching and instructions of an enlightened Master.

I thought of undertaking some research work for my Ph.D., so I registered in the University. I had a very learned Professor as my research supervisor; he was Dr. Advaita Mahanty, who was also my teacher during my career as a student. He had done his studies in Wisconsin, in the United States. He was a remarkable teacher and both inspired and helped me. I spent a lot of money and a lot of time for my research work. When my Ph.D. work was nearing its completion, I had a feeling that in this respect, Gurudev's words might not come true. But I was wrong.

During that time, everything drastically changed in my life. Gurudev convinced me to come to the West. I accepted and will narrate how it happened later on. I came to the West for some months and later when I went back to India, Baba initiated me into monastic life. So I left my job as well as my unfinished Ph.D. work. I gave all my notes and all my papers to my supervisor, who pleaded with me to stay two to three months more to complete the work before I left. He asked, "Will your Guruji not allow you to do this?" But I thought, 'What would I do with a Ph.D. degree?' That was the end of my Ph.D.

There was another occasion, in those early days, in which he forecast my future. One day, in the year 1984, some American disciples were taking a video of Shri Gurudev on the premises of the Puri Ashram. I was passing

1. Baba, as I first saw him in this life

2. My first photo with Baba, 1983

3. Baba and me with my friend Manoranjan, who was initiated with me

4. Baba on his way to the Jagannath Temple on March 23rd, 1986

5. In the Karar Ashram

6. The divine teacher

7. Baba in Cuttack at Dr. Niranjan Pradhan's house

by when I noticed the videotaping, and I quickly turned back. But Gurudev, who had already seen me, called out my name loudly and so I was forced to approach him. At that time I was very shy and did not talk much. He caught hold of my arm and said to the American disciples, "Look at this young man and take pictures. He looks very young but he is very, very old. One day he will go to America to teach meditation to you all." I was really embarrassed. I did not know much about meditation and I was a new student. What was he really saying? It could be that he was trying to encourage a young disciple. Now when I am in America, trying to carry out his mission, I remember his prediction of long ago and how his words came true. Gurudev's clear-cut vision has never ceased to amaze me.

In spiritual life, as a special discipline, every student should try to serve the Guru. By serving the Guru, one's own ego goes down. The Guru is the reflection through which one can look at one's own self. The Guru is the mirror, which points out mistakes. If one lives near the Guru and serves him, one's ego will diminish, the inner mind will be purified and the whole being will expand, in love. I stayed with Gurudev in the Ashram and served him as much as I could. There is a saying that God is like a mother-in-law and we are like daughters-in-law; when the daughter-in-law is pregnant, the mother-in-law gives her more rest and tells her not to work too much because she is carrying a child. Similarly, God gives more opportunity to meditate to one who sincerely meditates and prays to God.

Commuting Back and Forth

In the course of time, during 1986, by the grace of God, I was transferred from Rourkela to Cuttack. The Principal, when he heard about the transfer order, called me to his office and said that he was not happy about my leaving Rourkela. He offered that if I wanted to stay there, he would make all the arrangements to cancel my transfer orders. But if I wanted to go to Cuttack he would not be an impediment. I replied sincerely that I loved life in Rourkela, as I loved the work and the students, but

Cuttack was nearer to Puri where my Gurudev lived and above all I wanted to stay with my Gurudev. He blessed me and let me go. While in Cuttack, I had the opportunity to be with Gurudev longer and longer. I stayed in the Ashram permanently and commuted back and forth to Cuttack. It was about sixty miles from Puri to Cuttack. My classes would start almost every day early in the morning at about 7.00 a.m. and I had to leave the Ashram at 4.00 a.m. to reach Cuttack on time. I would teach and again I would come back to the Ashram in the afternoon, about 1 o'clock. Although it was a hectic schedule, I enjoyed it because of the love I received from Gurudev and the blessing of his company. One day Gurudev asked me, "Why do you take so much physical strain and spend so much money, coming to the Ashram everyday? You could come here on the weekends to meditate and go back during the week. You would avoid unnecessary physical and financial strain." I answered humbly, "Gurudev, money will come and go, physical strain is nothing to me, but your company is more valuable to me than anything else. I get so much joy, inner peace and spiritual progress in my life when I am with you, that is why I stay here." So Baba accepted my decision. He showed me in many ways how much he loved his disciples. He knew that I didn't eat food outside. I would come back from Cuttack and eat in the Ashram. Everyday, while he was taking food, in a special bowl he would set some food aside from his own plate. In Indian spiritual tradition, we consider the food from the plate of the Guru as *prasad,* or holy consecrated food. If anybody partakes of that food, they will obtain inner purification. He kept this special bowl in a special place, instructing other *brahmacharis* to keep it for me. After work, I would come back a little bit tired and hungry. The *brahmacharis* in the Ashram would come with the food saying, "Baba was asking when you would come back and he has set aside this food for you." When I heard that he inquired and thought of me and even kept food for me, all the discomfort and fatigue of the journey would disappear in an instant. Not only that, every night, when we bowed to him before he went to bed he would ask, "Baba, tomorrow at what time will you go to work?" I would reply, "4.00 a.m." and you would be surprised to know that every morning at quarter to four, he would come to my room and sit there and talk a little bit about meditation and spirituality. During these fifteen minutes, in my room, he would also check and make sure that I was dressed warmly enough for the winter and whether I had put an apple or some bananas in my bag for breakfast. Just like a loving and caring mother, he would come to the entrance of the Ashram to see me off. I would bow down again and he would bless me and say, "Come back safe." The Guru is like a caring and loving mother who looks after all the needs of her child. He takes care of the student in every aspect. By the grace of God, I had found such a loving Master. In the scriptures it is said, "There are many teachers, who look at a student to see what profit they can derive. But, the true Guru is the rarest of the rare, who steals the heart of the student." I saw the scriptures come alive in the love that emanated from the teacher-disciple relationship.

At that time I did not use a watch, but I was punctual in every activity. One day, I left the Ashram a little earlier than usual, before Baba came to my room. When I was a few steps away from the entrance and the *brahmacharis* were already closing the gate, Baba came and asked, "Has he left?" When he learnt that I had just left he said to them, "Call him back. If he doesn't see me before he goes, he may be unhappy on the way." Somebody shouted my name, "Triloki Baba come back, Baba is calling you." I came back and bowed down to him. Then he said, "In the Indian tradition, when one goes on a journey, you do not call him back. It is inauspicious. But when the mother or the Guru calls you back, it is a special blessing. So I bless you, you can go."

My days passed in the Ashram, serving Gurudev and he took care of his disciples in every way and helped us in our spiritual progress.

CHAPTER THREE

The Passage of Time

The wise spends time in intellectual discussion, the honest in truthful pursuit, the Yogi spends time in meditation, the king in conquest, the idle spends time in quarrels and conflict. You are as you spend your time.

Sanskrit Proverb

Guru is Omniscient

In India, people believe that the Guru is the living presence of God and as such is omniscient. He knows what we need and what we do. In one incident, Gurudev indirectly showed me that he knew the smallest of my movements. When I was working in Cuttack, Gurudev visited the town and stayed in a disciple's house in complete seclusion. Nobody was allowed to visit him. Though I was a little disappointed not to be able to see him, I was gratified that Baba could get some seclusion and rest. On the day Baba was to leave Cuttack for Puri, I telephoned to find out the time of his departure. I went to a disciple's house, close to work, to make the call. Gurudev asked if I had finished my work for the day and that he would be leaving in half an hour. I had to come over quickly so I could travel with him in the same car. As I was leaving my friend's house, his mother came out with four special *laddus,* Indian sweets made of sesame seeds, and with great love fed me one, put two in my pocket and placed another one in my hand to eat on the way. I was in a hurry. I ate the *laddu* while walking, and then gave the rest to my friend who drove me to where Gurudev was staying.

When we arrived, my friend who was also initiated into Kriya Yoga and worked at the same college, in the library, came in and we both bowed down to Baba. Baba said to him, "Do you know Triloki Baba can teach you meditation? He is empowered to initiate, he can initiate many among you, and then you all come and learn meditation from him." Gurudev once more predicted my future in the presence of others.

On the way to Puri, I was sitting in the front and Gurudev was sitting in the back. I wanted to turn my head and look at his face, but he was touching my head from the backseat and telling me where to concentrate in the fontanel. He was teaching me how to meditate with eyes open and I was following his instructions. A car passed us from the opposite direction. There was a monk sitting inside. Gurudev asked me if I had seen the monk sitting in the other car and eating something. I had not seen anything clearly as I was trying to meditate, therefore I was vague in my answer. So Baba told me a story about the life of an Indian king. The moral of that story was not to eat while walking. At the end, Gurudev said to me, "Listen, while walking on the street you should not eat food." I was really surprised, as no one has seen me eating the *laddu* while walking. In other words he was telling me that he was aware of my every movement, that I should avoid mistakes and follow the strict discipline of the scriptures.

Gurudev knew much about me. Long before I became aware, he knew the turns and twists I would find on the spiritual path. With his love and guidance, he shaped my life. Today, I am convinced the omniscient Guru knew the direction my life would take from the very start.

One afternoon, as we were to travel from Puri to Cuttack, Gurudev took his tiffin and tea before we left. It was a three hours trip by train. On the way, the train was unusually delayed and stopped a little distance away from a station. It was already dark and I had taken no food since morning. I was feeling extremely hungry. Just then Gurudev said to me, "Do you know I am feeling very hungry. Can you go over to the railway station and bring me some food? Biscuits would be good." I knew that this was the play of Gurudev, he knew that

I was hungry and wanted to feed me, Gurudev had already taken his tiffin. I hesitated, not very willing to walk nearly half a mile to bring some food. As I got down from the train, in the darkness, I walked a few steps and then decided to turn around. Just as I turned, I saw Gurudev standing near the door of the compartment, watching me. He could read my mind, and he knew that I might turn around and come back, so he stood near the door to make sure I would go. When I saw him, I turned back and walked straight to the railway station and bought some biscuits. I came back and handed the packet to him, he thanked me by saying, "Very nice," and he took one biscuit and ate it. Then he handed me the rest with a smile, "You eat because you are really hungry."

It is evident that Gurudev knows the mind and the thought pattern of his disciples. With these tools, he guides us to achieve our true potential. In another incident, while staying in the Ashram at Bhubaneshwar, Gurudev had left for Cuttack in a car. About a quarter of an hour later, Gurudev suddenly came back to the Ashram. He did not come inside, but sat in the car waiting for something. We were surprised that he had returned, but he said nothing. After some time, a European lady disciple reached the Ashram and got down from a rickshaw, Baba opened the door of the car and came out. She knelt and bowed down to him, Baba talked to her a little and blessed her. Then Baba said to her, "I came back from my trip to Cuttack, knowing that you were coming to see me and that you would be heartbroken and disappointed if you could not find me here. I could sense that you were having problems finding the Ashram." It turned out that the rickshaw puller was having a lot of trouble locating the Ashram, as the lady could not remember the exact name.

A Guru knows the mind and the heart of the disciple even from the distance; he can perceive things beyond the capacity of a normal human being. There are many means of communication between the Guru and his disciples. A look might replace speech or talk, and in the distance a Guru can join his disciple through thought, or prayer.

Holi, The Color Festival

In the month of March, in India, there is the celebration of *Holi*. On this festival, people put color powder on each other to commemorate the divine play of Krishna and the joyful way he would have fun with his friends.

On such an occasion Gurudev was also in a playful mood. As he emerged from his room he suggested to his disciples to apply color to his feet. We were all overjoyed. Then he suggested we put color all over him. Suddenly Gurudev had become Krishna, as playful and full of laughter. Then we all sang together with devotion.

It took Baba quite some time to get rid of all the traces of colored powder but it left us with an indelible memory of a day full of fun and joy.

My First Letter

When Gurudev went away, I thought of him frequently. I felt a strong wish to write to him and keep in touch. It was in 1986, that filled with courage, I wrote my first letter and sent it to America, where Gurudev was staying. Everyday I expected a reply. After what seemed like a long time, I was sitting with one of my colleagues, who was also one of my professors and she said, "Do you know Triloki, there was an envelope that was addressed to you without any sender's name on it. But I think there was nothing in that envelope. It was so thin. Maybe somebody posted it by mistake. I brought the envelope for you." After searching for it for a while, she found the letter and gave it to me. It was an Indian envelope, with unfamiliar handwriting. I knew everyone who wrote to me, on a regular basis and could recognize the handwriting. When I opened the envelope, there was a small thin piece of paper, which was actually the letter Baba had sent to me. Usually when Gurudev writes letters to India, he writes to many disciples at a time and then sends all the contents to one disciple for distribution. When I got the letter there were tears in my eyes and such joy in my face, so that my colleague looked at me in astonishment. When I shared with her the small piece of paper she was moved by the beauty of its contents. I proudly told her that he was my Guru. That was my first letter from Gurudev and later on I made it a practice to write him every week. Whether Gurudev replied or not, it did not matter, if a letter of mine would reach his hand, he would remember me, surely this would help in my spiritual evolution. From that time onwards, I have written countless letters to Gurudev and have treasured all his replies.

Even in the distance, I felt very close to my Guru. When he did not answer my letters, sometimes I would become anxious. When Gurudev was in America in 1992, I wrote to him several times but there was no reply. One day, after my prayers and meditation, I went to work. When I came back, many student disciples were waiting for me. Although I lived in a rented house, everybody knew it to be an Ashram. As soon as I returned, they circled around me excitedly, "Baba, Baba, what will you give us in return if we present you with something very special?" For a moment I stopped to think what would have caused such upheaval. Then I asked, "Is there any letter from Gurudev?" Seconds later, I received the long-waited reply. Gurudev had dictated it and a disciple from Holland had written a letter on behalf of Baba. In it the following words could be read, "Please don't be unhappy that I have not replied to you. It is because of my health, I am not able to write. I am always with you, I always remember you, I am praying for you everyday." The Dutch disciple added a few words of her own, explaining to me how Baba constantly told her how much I loved Gurudev and how unhappy I would be if I did not receive any news. A Guru's love knows no bounds.

His Vision

In 1987, Gurudev said to me, "Baba why don't you purchase a small piece of land by the river side and have an Ashram there?" At that time I had a clear rejection of all material things. I thought this was a way in which Gurudev wanted to test me. An Ashram would mean land, building, property and above all a lot of responsibility. I did not need all this. I remained silent. He repeated the same instructions several times, but I did not pay any heed. In 1992, five years later, due to certain circumstances, I ended up purchasing a small piece of land, very close to the river and started an Ashram there. It is the present Cuttack Ashram. Baba had foreseen its creation many years before. His words and his vision came true. On the 17th of May, 1993, we inaugurated the Cuttack Ashram. The Guru had long since had the vision of the direction my life would take in the future.

A Guru Kills Ego

Gurudev wants to crush our ego. One day I was serving Gurudev, sitting in his room in the Puri Ashram taking dictation. I had a cold and a runny nose, so I held a handkerchief to my nose with one hand and I wrote with the other. Baba was aware of my difficulty and said to me, "If I tell you to do something, will you follow me?" This was really a difficult question to answer without knowing what he would ask. I looked at him. He repeated, "Tell me if you want to follow me or not?" Hesitantly I said, "Yes". Then he told me to open his bag and take out some cold medicine. Finally, he instructed me to take two tablets immediately. I took the tablets but kept them in my pocket. This is where my ego came up. I had been very sick in my childhood and I was always dependant on medicines, but since 1979, I had taken no medicines. I thought I did not need any medicine since I was a Yogi. Gurudev knew about this and wanted to remove my ego. I wanted to leave the room on the pretext of getting some water, so I could come back without taking the medicine. As though he read my mind, Gurudev said to me, "No need to go out" and gave me his glass of water. I swallowed the medicine for my cold and for my ego. A Guru knows not only our mind, he knows the cause of our ego and he wants to remove it, to help us grow spiritually. I learnt a valuable lesson.

The Prophecy

At another time Gurudev asked me, "If some spiritual organizations would invite you, would you go there or not?" "What for?" I asked. He said, "If they invite you to speak at their functions and celebrations, would you go or not?" At that time I was leading the life of a contemplative person and did not speak anywhere, on any spiritual topic, so I said, "If somebody invites me and if it is for a good purpose, it would be a good gesture to accept that invitation." He seemed pleased, "Would you talk about Kriya Yoga or about other topics?" I was wondering what type of test he was putting me through. I answered, "If another spiritual organization is inviting me to give a talk on a specific occasion, why should I talk about Kriya Yoga?" He looked very interested, "Then what will you talk about?" I replied, "The teachings of Gurudev without naming specifically Kriya Yoga; a practical way to spirituality and how to love God by making changes in our life and activities. If I am ever invited, I would talk about this." I was actually surprised when some time later I was invited by several reputed spiritual organizations to give talks. By the grace of God and Gurus, who spoke through me, I began to give talks and lectures in many places. Then I remembered what Gurudev said before my initiation, "Many spiritual organizations will invite you." Nowadays, when I give a talk, I remember Gurudev's omniscience, his future forecasting and his training. He encouraged me to gain scriptural knowledge by reading books and to maintain a meditative outlook. He instructed me on how to balance scriptural knowledge with meditation. Through practice, I gained experience.

His Teaching

One day after lunch, everybody including Gurudev, was taking a nap in the Ashram. I was lying down in the verandah of the Temple of Shriyukteshwar, reading a beautiful spiritual book, written by the brother disciple of Gurudev's first Guru, Vijay Krishna. The name of the book was *Sadhana Samar*, the metaphorical interpretation of *Durga Saptasati*, by Brahmarshi Satyadev. Gurudev came out of his room and was walking around, very silently he approached the Temple and stood there. I could always tell when Gurudev was near, by the special fragrance that emanated from him. I sat up and he looked at me with a smile and asked, "Which book are you reading?" I showed him the book. Then he said, "Please read aloud." It was written in Bengali. I read out to him and he listened carefully. After a paragraph he insisted, "No need to read any more, just sit silently and meditate. Don't read only. Through reading, you will get only book knowledge. Read and meditate. When both factors are joined, you will require more spiritual evolution, insight and experience." Then Baba sat there with me and we both meditated for about fifteen minutes. After this he suggested, "Again you read a little." This is how he trained me in reading the scriptures and meditation. He also encouraged me to study in depth the Bible, the Koran, the Upanishads, and the Bhagavad Gita. Many times he tested my understanding. Often he would ask, "What do you think of this verse? What is its meaning?" With his careful guidance, I learnt to go deeply into the meaning of many verses. Through Gurudev's teaching I gained insight, which I am able to use in turn to guide others.

The Test

Around 1986, Gurudev carried out a most unusual test on me. I shared a room with the present Swami Brahmanandaji, who at that time was known as Ray Baba. He had great affection for me and I loved his purity and silent nature. During that time my parents, my brothers and sister were all visiting the Ashram, since they had all become disciples of Shri Gurudev. Taking advantage of this, Baba called me and said, "I want to make you Lahiri Mahasaya." When Baba talks, he talks many times metaphorically. I was not able to understand what he meant by making me Lahiri Mahasaya, so I was thoughtful. After a couple of hours, Baba pointed out to a young lady and said, "Is it not good to marry her?" I was taken aback. What could he want, but I didn't say anything, I just left the place. I was really unhappy with his remark and reflected, "Why is he saying this to me? Is it my destiny to get married? And if it is my destiny, then why don't I feel any urge to get married? Is he really omniscient and he knows what I need? Does he know my destiny?" Needless to say I was both confused and upset. As Ray Baba and I were sharing a bedroom at that time, I turned to him and I was literally crying and repeating, "Why does Baba speak like this?" That night I really could not sleep. The next day Baba started talking about the same topic and my confusion augmented, "Do you know she is working. So you will have less responsibility and can meditate more." I was unhappy and decided that if anyone forced me to marry against my will, I would leave that person. Forget the Guru, I would make my own way. Certainly I had no need to marry. I recalled a song that Tulsi Das, a great poet saint of India, wrote to Meera, a famous lady saint, instructing her that if anyone was a hindrance on the spiritual path, even if that person was your own Guru or parents, a close friend or a husband, one should leave them without hesitation. At the same time I felt tormented, how could I leave my chosen Guru? He was a major force in my life and I had accepted him after a lot of trials and tribulations, with so much conviction. But why would I have to marry? The second night, I also spent in a sleepless fashion and close to tears. Additionally, I became apprehensive about my family, who were visiting the Ashram at that time. They might be happy to see Gurudev persuading me to lead a family life. The next day Ray Baba proposed, "Why don't you talk with Baba directly?" We both went to Baba's room. Ray Baba told him that I wanted to ask him something. Baba looked at me. It was morning time. He had finished his breakfast and he said to me, "What do you want to ask me?" I looked at him without answering. He insisted, "Please tell me. What do you want to ask me?" He was asking with love, but I had tears in my eyes and I could not say what I wanted to say. He looked at Ray Baba and asked him, "He is not saying anything, what does he want to say?" Then Ray Baba explained the source of trouble, "Why does Gurudev tell him repeatedly to marry?" Immediately Baba reacted, "Oh! That is the reason why he is unhappy? I was only playing with him." I did not understand why my Guruji played like this. Was it to test my mind or to see the strength of my determination?

My Mother's Reply

Although the members of my family were already initiated, I never felt the need to introduce them to Gurudev. They had no special treatment, they came, spent a few days in meditation, enjoyed the company of Gurudev, and then they left again.

As I returned from my job, one afternoon, I went in search of Gurudev. I was told that he was with some of the devotees near the Samadhi Temple, the shrine of Shriyukteshwarji. As I made my way I saw my mother and some of my relatives along with other people, forming a small circle around Gurudev. My mother was sitting close to Baba. Since I was shy, my first thought was to turn around, go to my room and change my clothes.

Gurudev, who knew my mind and how I would react, called me back. So I was forced to approach the group. I bowed down to my mother first and then to my Guru. The other disciples were somewhat curious, eagerly waiting to know who she was. Immediately Gurudev said, "She is my Divine Mother; the mother of a Jewel." He went on to explain to my mother the high hopes he had for me in the spiritual field.

The next day my mother was with Gurudev and with two other relatives, Baba asked her, "Why don't you think of the marriage of your son Triloki?" My mother looked at him earnestly and replied, "Gurudev, you know everything. Knowingly, why do you ask me that question? I have five children. Out of the five, I have given you one. So you are to see what is best for him and you are to guide him. I am not worried whether he will be married or not." Gurudev was happy to hear her confirmation. Later on he added, "You will never speak to him about marriage. If you do, then he will be very unhappy and he will not come to see you so frequently." From that time onwards, my mother relied on my Guru and told me to serve him with complete devotion.

On another occasion, a long time disciple of Gurudev, who was socially in a very respected position, was visiting him. He had a young daughter and had a plan in mind. Taking my hand and showing it to Gurudev, he said, "Please look at this hand, is there a *sannyas* line on his hand, which would indicate the life of a monk or will he be a householder? If you predict he would be a monk as Shriyukteshwar predicted about you, then let him be a monk. If not he can be a good householder, we can arrange for his marriage." I was silent. Gurudev took my hand and looking at my hand he said playfully, "He is already married. How many times can he get married?" He was very pleased at the effect of his statement and added, "He is already married to me, to the service of God and Gurus. Once he is married to Hariharananda, he would not want to marry again." With this he meant that I would not be a householder, although it was put in such a humorous way. I was both happy and relieved. I bowed down to him and left the room. I loved Gurudev so much, I often thought of him as my mother and my father. To me the path of spirituality was clearly my path, as I had no wish for worldly life.

A retired Principal of a school was a longtime disciple of Gurudev and was paying him a visit. When he saw a few young men like myself, all bachelors, he said, "Gurudev! There is a proverb: 'bachelors live like kings and die like dogs', since they have no one to look after them in their old age." Gurudev immediately remarked, "You are wrong. If the bachelor in question leads a spiritual life he will live like a king and die like a king. Do you not know that the monks and *brahmacharis* are addressed here in India as 'Maharajji'. That means 'Your Majesty'. If a bachelor lives a self-disciplined life, he will also die like a king, loved by people during his lifetime and equally revered after he leaves his body. On the other hand, ordinary householders, keeping their mind immersed in material activities, far from God, are always restless, stressed and often disturbed. Their life is often full of unhappiness and tension. Their life is not so beautiful since their main duty is to watch over their family."

Remain on Top and Watch Yourself

During my apprenticeship, I freely went to Baba's room and would sit near him, talk to him and listen to him. One day as I was entering his room, he was looking at a big clock with a pendulum hanging on the wall. He signaled to me with his fingers to come close to him. I went near him. He said, "Listen to the clock. What does the clock say?" I looked at the clock, unable to understand the meaning of the question. I only heard the sound of 'tick, tack'. Baba placed his finger on the top of my head and said, "The clock is saying '*dekh, dekh, dekh*', which in English means 'watch, watch, watch'. In every breath, at every moment, watch the indwelling Self. Do not waste a single moment." Gurudev taught me in every step of life how to love God more, to remain in the higher planes, always on top, in the fontanel. He taught me how to live permanently immersed in God-consciousness.

A great spiritual Master of our time, also taught in a verse,

> "Watch your Words
> Watch your Action
> Watch your Thought
> Watch your Character
> Watch your Heart."

To Travel and to Serve

In January 1986, I traveled with Gurudev to Western Orissa. We went to Rourkela, Bhavanipatna, Jharsuguda and Sambalpur. I felt fortunate to be in the company of my Master and to be able to serve him. While we were in Bhavanipatna, Gurudev was giving dictation to some disciples for the evening program. As I entered his room, I heard Baba saying, "The opening song is by Triloki Baba". I was very surprised. He looked at me and said, "Yes, I know. Triloki Baba cannot sing. Triloki Baba will not sing, Hariharananda will sing through Triloki Baba". Up to that time I always thought that Gurudev was unaware that I loved to sing.

In my innermost being I have often felt that life is a song, unfortunately very few know how to sing the song of life. Life, when viewed as a song, opens up the heart and brings inner love.

As a child, I was often with my mother, who happened to be very pious, always singing devotional and spiritual songs. I learnt singing from her, so I have considered this an inner gift from my mother. In my leisure time I would often sing devotional songs and my mother would encourage me to learn more. She enjoyed to hear me sing.

That evening I had to sing a yogic song in Oriya, which compares the human body to an inverted tree. This also happens to be one of Baba's favorite songs. When I started singing, Baba would sometimes join in. From that time onwards he always encouraged me to sing devotional and spiritual songs. It has been proved to me again and again that Baba knows the innermost personality of a being.

Traveling with Baba on a train had unusual moments. On that very trip, coming back from Bhavanipatna to Rourkela, Baba refused to go into his assigned compartment. I, who was carrying his bags, became worried. We had no other reservations. This did not bother Gurudev at all. He told me to talk to the ticket controller, who found a sleeping berth for Baba. I spent the whole night sitting in a corner, looking at Baba and trying to meditate with my eyes open. Sometimes I managed to get a little sleep. When we reached Rourkela, the next morning at 4 o'clock, there were around fifty disciples waiting for Gurudev. When we reached our destination we all sat for meditation and Gurudev began to guide while I dozed off. As soon as he noticed it, he told me to go and rest, but I did not want to miss one second of his presence and guidance. I made a big effort to control my need for sleep and continued to meditate. Through small sacrifices one learns self-control. In time I have learnt to control my sleeping pattern so that I could fit more work during my wakeful hours.

To stay with the Master, to be with him, is a rare opportunity. I feel blessed to have shared so many moments in Puri, Cuttack, Bhubaneshwar, Rourkela, Sambalpur, Calcutta and Madras, in Europe and in America. All I know I have learnt from Gurudev. Traveling and serving him has been a divine opportunity.

Swami Triloki

In September 1987, I finally felt ready to organize a program for Gurudev in Cuttack. Cuttack was a place I knew well since I had both studied and worked there. Many old disciples of Gurudev lived in this area. A public address struck me as a good idea, so I expressed my wish, "Baba, I would like to organize a public program. Would Baba kindly permit me to organize it and bless this occasion with his presence and address this program?" Gurudev agreed, and suggested Ms. Manorama Mahapatra, the Associate Editor of the most popular newspaper, 'The Samaj', to preside over the function. She happened to be my ex-professor and kindly consented.

The date of the program was fixed. The hall was packed with people. A few friends of mine were involved in the organization.

Gurudev had already arrived, but there was no microphone. It was the month of September, there was a celebration of *Ganesh Puja*, the lord of wisdom and success. Every educational institution and public place in Cuttack was celebrating this event and many microphones and sound systems were being used, all over the city. I could not get a microphone. I did not know what to do. Gurudev was already there. Without a microphone, who could hear him? Among the audience, a friend, aware of my dilemma went out, and to my great relief came back with a microphone. When the microphone was ready and the sound system was set up, just at that moment the Associate Editor entered the room and the program started. I was so relieved to see that everything went well.

During the program, Ms. Mahapatra, referred to me as 'Swami Triloki', her beloved student. This touched Baba's heart. Later, on several occasions, Gurudev said to me, "Do you remember the day your professor Manorama Mahapatra referred to you as 'Swami Triloki'? So she knows that you will become a Swami but I know that you will not become a Swami since you are already a Swami." He would joke repeatedly, "You are a Swami, you are a Swami, and you are a monk, more than a monk." And later on he made me a monk.

The Start of Initiation

In the beginning of 1992, Gurudev was in Jharsaguda, a town in Western Orissa. He asked me to come to his room. That morning there were nearly sixty people ready to be initiated. When I went to his room, he told me to close the door. I sat down near his feet. Finally, he demanded, "Why are you not following me?" I remained silent, so he continued, "Why are you still unwilling to initiate people?" I just looked at him. I was not really willing to initiate people for two specific reasons. When one starts initiating in spiritual life, many times one gets the ego of being spiritually advanced. Spiritual ego is extremely dangerous. Perhaps it is the most dangerous ego of all. I was meditating only for my own spiritual progress. Apart from that, I did not feel yet ready to take on the responsibility of other people, by initiating them. My relationship with my Guru was to meditate and become spiritually enlightened.

Although Gurudev was encouraging me to initiate since 1987 onwards, I was always reluctant. But that day Gurudev became insistent, "If you do not follow me, do you think you will get spiritual progress? I am telling you that if you follow my direction you will get spiritual evolution. Do you think a Guru does not know what is good for his disciple? Do you think that I do not want your all-round development? Please! Today I will not take a 'no' for an answer. Do not sit silently. Accept my offer and my advice. Tell me, will you follow your Guru or not?" It was a critical question. To follow the Guru it is not always easy, yet there can be nothing more and nothing less. That day I knew I could not say 'no' to him. He also knew so he added, "You meditate here for a while and then go and initiate." He did not even show me how to initiate or what the *mantras* were to be used in the ceremony. The omniscient Guru knew that I knew all these *mantras* because I sat near him for a long period of time while he was initiating and guiding many disciples. It was his conviction that I had already absorbed all these things. I bowed down to him after meditation and started the first of many initiations. After initiation, the new disciples would bow down to Baba and seek his blessings. Gurudev would ask them about their experience during initiation. After it was all over I also went to bow down to Baba, and to my joy he hugged me and kissed me and said, "I am so happy that today you did not say 'no'. Today you followed me. My blessings and my love will be always with you. There is no question about it. All the people you initiated got extreme calmness and inner experience of divine light, sound and vibration. Meditate sincerely and your fear of getting ego and losing spiritual power, will never happen to you. I bless you. I will be always with you. You are not initiating, I will be initiating through you." This is how he convinced me to start initiating. My path lay more and more clearly before me.

Family Duty

One day Gurudev gave me a good amount of money. Usually, when I stayed with Gurudev in the Ashram, if somebody was to be given money, for charity, Gurudev would give me the amount and I would be in charge of handing it to the concerned person. But this day Gurudev instructed me to keep it with me. I was surprised and I asked Baba for whom the money was intended. He did not reply, he just instructed me to keep the funds available. Since I never accepted money, without knowing the purpose for which it was intended, I asked him again. Only then did he reply with the following words, "Do you know my mother has no teeth in her mouth and she has difficulties in eating. I want dentures to be made for my mother." When Baba was saying my mother, he was pointing to my own mother. I looked at him with tears in my eyes and said, "Baba, I am her son, but I couldn't recognize her difficulty. You are the Guru who is to teach the student and guide him in the right way. In spite of being her son, I was not aware of the trouble my mother was going through until you pointed it out to me. That is enough, I have money, Baba. I can do this for my mother. Please don't force me to take money. I can do this on my own." Gurudev was satisfied and instructed me to go ahead with the project. When I suggested it to my mother, she declined to have new teeth as it was a really unusual thing to do for people living in a village. Then Gurudev, who had already left for America, sent many letters and at the end a cassette, in which he gave practical spiritual instruction and also inquired about my mother and her teeth. I brought the cassette and played it to my mother while trying to convince her, "We should all follow our Guruji. Why are you still unwilling, if Baba is so concerned? Finally my mother agreed and she came to stay with me for a good period of time in Cuttack, while she had her dentures made. Some time later, when Baba was passing through Cuttack, he saw my mother at the railway-station, and remarked how beautiful she looked. A true Guru not only teaches us spirituality, he also guides us in our social and family life that we can love and serve our parents and family in a better way. Gurudev himself gave us the example when he continued serving his own mother and father even though he was a monk. Gurudev encouraged me to occasionally write to my mother, to talk with her over the telephone so that she did not feel abandoned or neglected by her son.

His Training

Lahiri Mahasaya had a disciple, a householder Yogi, Panchanan Bhattacharya, whom he always addressed as 'Pundita', which means the learned or the wise one. He was not only a great scholar in Sanskrit, but also an advanced Yogi. Panchanan Bhattacharya always took note of Lahiri Mahasaya's teachings and later on printed these texts for the benefit of all other disciples.

While I was a *brahmachari*, Baba would also affectionately call me 'Pundita'. Whenever there was any scriptural reference to be verified, Baba would say, "Call the Pundita" and then would ask me for the reference in question. Even when he was in the West, he would often write letters asking me to search for this or that scriptural quotation and its reference. During those early years in the company of Gurudev, it became a regular habit during his talks that he would start a verse and I would be instructed to complete it. Sometimes, Gurudev would suggest a chapter and the title and would glance meaningfully at me, and I would quote the verse completely. Other times while quoting a verse, he would look at me and ask me what scripture the verse came from. Finally, one day Gurudev was addressing a public gathering. I was busy outside the hall, organizing last minute details but at the same time I was trying to listen to his conference. While giving his talk, he stopped and started to look for me to complete the verse. Immediately I rushed inside and concluded the verse. Baba said triumphantly to the audience, "You see without him I am incomplete. He and I are one. What is started by me has to be completed by him."

Gurudev told us a few anecdotes of his early days with Shriyukteshwarji. Shriyukteshwarji would always keep a pocket sized Gita with him. During a discourse, when he needed a reference from the Gita, he would just open the book, but when Gurudev was there, he would quote the verse with reference from his memory, to set an example.

Due to the thorough training that I received from Gurudev, I was able to remember and understand the inner meaning of the scriptures and also memorize various *mantras*, prayers and ritualistic practices. His teaching and exhaustive training were a silent preparation for the future.

His Protective Foresight

In 1986 there was a *Kumbha Mela* in Hardwar. That year I had a lot of vacation and I stayed as much as I could with Gurudev in different Ashrams. I also booked a train ticket to Hardwar, to attend the *Kumbha Mela,* which was scheduled for the month of April.

Kumbha Mela is a spiritual festival in India, and is celebrated in four holy places, two in Northern India in Hardwar and Allahabad on the banks of *Ganga* and the other two in Central India, one in Ujjain and the other in Nasik. It takes place between the months of January and September, at three years intervals, by rotation. This means it is repeated in the same place every twelve years. At the *Kumbha Mela* thousands of monks, spiritual persons and millions of people from all over the world congregate. Monks of different orders, and different monastic traditions gather there. Many spiritual discussions and spiritual activities take place. In India it is considered auspicious to go there, partake in the holy gathering and bathe in the holy river.

Kumbha Mela has a mythological origin. The literal meaning of *kumbha* is a pitcher and *mela* means festival. According to Hindu mythology, the gods and demons churned the ocean of milk, from which a pitcher of ambrosia came out. Those who drank the nectar would be free from all suffering and achieve immortality. The gods did not want to share this nectar with the demons so they kept a pitcher hidden in each of these four places. A few drops of nectar fell on these four places, so the *Kumbha*

Mela is celebrated to commemorate this event. The exact time depends upon astrological calculation.

I booked my ticket to go to Hardwar, not saying a word about my plan to anyone. Yet Gurudev began to sound apprehensive, "There is no need to go to the *Kumbha Mela*. Your body is a pitcher or pot and this body should be cleaned from within. Everyone hides anger, pride, jealousy, hypocrisy, cruelty and ego, all negative qualities, which become poison. Love, purity, sincerity, simplicity and compassion are nectar. One should clean the pot of his own life and remove all the poisonous elements of anger and ego, and should fill his life with the nectar of love and purity." This is what the *Kumbha Mela* really is. A yogic scripture tells,

āmakumbha ivāmbhasi, jīrnamāna sadā ghataḥ
yogānalena saṃdahya ghata sudhiṃ samācaret

"This body is an unbaked clay pot, dissolving when in touch with the water of sense organs and worldly affairs. When burnt and purified by the fire, the body becomes strong and can withstand the world of objects. We should transform our life through the practice of Yoga."

Gheranda Samhita I.8

Each human body is like an unbaked pitcher. When the pitcher is not burnt or baked in the fire, it will dissolve when it comes in contact with water. Similarly, the human body cannot find peace while being submerged in the world of objects and the ocean of desires, unless it is burnt and purified by the practice of Yoga and meditation. The body pot should be cleaned and baked. A bath in the holy rivers is only a ritual, unless the mind is made pure. It became obvious that Gurudev was discouraging me from going to the *Kumbha Mela*. I cancelled my ticket, Baba had persuaded me that, for the time being, I should focus more on meditation than on visiting holy places.

To my surprise, during that particular *Kumbha Mela,* there was a great accident and hundreds of people died crushed, due to a stampede. I did not know the will of God and Gurus, but I am convinced that the omniscient Guru prevented me from visiting this *Kumbha Mela* and helped me to transform my life, through meditation. Without any doubt, visiting holy places is good but transforming our life through meditation is even better.

A Real Economist

Gurudev always made fun about my being a real economist, since I was a teacher of Economics at that time. When I was a student, and even while I was working, I used to shave my head clean three to four times a year. It was very comfortable for me, but I knew that Baba did not like this, so I usually took advantage of his absence, during summer vacation or *puja* vacation, when he traveled to the West. Once, during one of these intervals in September or October, I had nearly a month's holiday and I shaved my head. Baba came back to India unexpectedly. We received him at the airport. When we were all in a mini bus, going back to the Ashram, Baba looked at me and asked, "What is the reason for shaving your head?" I told him, "Baba, it is very comfortable. I do not need to go to the barbershop so frequently, for three to four months I do not go at all, and there is no need of using oil, soap or shampoo. I do not need to spend so much time, combing my hair, in front of the mirror." He looked at me, smiled and said, "You are a real economist. You know how to calculate and spend money so nicely, so wisely." It was his favorite joke. At another time, he cautioned me not to spend so much money traveling wherever he was, in Calcutta, or Puri, or Rourkela. Instead I should save money for my future or stay comfortably at home, meditating. My reply was always the same, "Baba this is a good investment. In this investment whatever is invested, will come back in huge return. People invest money in stocks and shares, I am investing time in good company, in my Guru's company." He would laugh and say, "You are a real economist. Surely whatever you are investing will come back to you manifold."

Becoming His Mouthpiece

Gurudev is an ocean of wisdom. His approach, his talk, his interpretation, everything is unique. During my first years in the company of Gurudev, I listened intently, but from 1984 onwards, I started taking notes. Later on, with the help of a tape recorder, I tried to record all his talks and conversations. When Gurudev was not in India, I would transcribe these tapes, observe silence, meditate, and listen again, wholeheartedly, to every syllable. This became my special project during the holidays. In this way I transcribed hundreds of cassettes. I was fascinated by his teaching methods and the depth of his interpretation.

At first I misunderstood him, because I was not able to comprehend the subtlety of his teachings. When he quoted the Upanishads and other yogic scriptures, I thought that he wanted to bring everything down to Kriya Yoga, and that he used the scriptures just to highlight Kriya Yoga. He quoted a beautiful verse from the Mundaka Upanishad (II.1.8), that means,

sapta-prāṇāḥ prabhavanti tasmāt
saptārciṣas samidhas sapta-homāḥ
sapta ime lokā yeṣu caranti prāṇā
guhāśayā nihitās sapta sapta

"From him come forth the seven life-breaths, the seven flames, their fuel, the seven oblations, these seven worlds in which move the life-breaths, seven and seven which dwell in the secret place in the divine path (in the spine and brain)."

I realized my mistake. Infinite is the stupidity of the disciple and infinite is the grace of the Guru. It was an education to see that what Gurudev taught was completely correct according to the scriptures.

On the 27th of May, 1987, we had a surprise birthday celebration for Gurudev in the Puri Ashram and I talked for the first time in his presence. In that special program many disciples from Orissa and Bengal were present. Debi Baba, the beloved nephew of Gurudev and his first disciple, was highly complementary of my first effort. Referring to me and my talk, he said to Baba, "He has swallowed, digested and assimilated you completely in his brain."

To speak to an audience, in the presence of Gurudev, is a very difficult task. He interrupts the talk and points out, slowly whispering near your ear, what you should say and how you should say it. To take Gurudev's ideas and incorporate them into the talk is an additional effort, but a beautiful training. He encouraged me to always speak in many languages; in Bengali, in Hindi, in Oriya and sometimes in English. Once this first step was taken, I began to give a series of talks in the presence of Gurudev. While in Calcutta I spoke in Bengali, in Jarsaguda, Orissa I spoke in Hindi and in Bhawanipatna I spoke in Oriya. Curiously, in Bhawanipatna, he did not allow anybody else to speak. When he asked me to take the floor, I was unaware that he was holding a tape recorder and recording the entire speech. It was more than one hour and fifteen minutes long. At the end, he showed his approval by stating, "There is no need for anybody else to speak. I will request everybody to please make a copy of this cassette and listen to it again and again. He has said everything about Hariharananda and his teachings, there is nothing further to say." I bowed down at his feet with complete surrender. I thanked him for his inspiration and training and his encouragement to give talks and to start writing about his teachings. To this day, he sits near his monks and he listens to our talk silently, in Vienna, in Calcutta, in America. When I teach any class on the Bible, on the Gita, or on any other topic, he will come in silently and he will listen, then when I have finished and we are alone he will comment on what I should have stressed more. He is the author and I am his open book. His words come down through me. When I speak, as when I write, I feel I am a tool of words and wisdom far greater than my own.

CHAPTER FOUR

Drawing me to the West

yastu pravrajate deśān yastu seveta panditān tasya sancāritā buddhiḥ taila vindumivāmbhasi.

One who travels around the world, one who serves the wise, has a very vast periphery of knowledge, as a drop of oil spills over a pot of water.

Sanskrit Proverb

For a long time Gurudev inwardly encouraged and prepared me to come and live in the West. He would frequently comment about the differences in clothing and in habits, between the East and the West, since he was aware of my preference for a simple lifestyle. Through conversation, he made me familiar with Western life and values. Baba also inspired me to study and interpret the Bible with a meditative outlook.

From my childhood, I had the vision that I would come to the West. Gradually, as I entered a strict spiritual life, under the guidance of Gurudev, it became clearer to me that I might come to the West not as an academician, but as a spiritual teacher. From the very start, Gurudev had predicted my coming to the West. Often he would correct my English pronunciation. At that time I spoke very fast and he would say, "If you speak so fast others will not be able to understand you. Especially when you come to Europe, you should speak very slowly and distinctly, making adequate pauses. He spoke from his own experience, as he himself had faced innumerable difficulties on this subject and had had to train himself. Since I was still in my twenties, I used to wonder why he was in such a hurry that I should travel to Europe and to America. Later on, when I became a teacher of Kriya Yoga, he became even more insistent. He asked me repeatedly to get my passport ready and wrote many letters to this purpose.

I was not really willing to come to the West. There were three things, which I did not want to do. The first was that I did not want to become a teacher of Kriya Yoga. As I mentioned earlier, I was afraid of developing ego and taking on the burden of others through initiation. Secondly, I was unwilling to come to the West. I had seen Gurudev bring many disciples to the West and how for some reason or another they did not meet his expectations. I was in no rush, if I was meant to go, it would be after the age of fifty. Gurudev had come to the West when he was sixty-seven years old. I myself would come to the West after fifty, not before that. The third strong objection I had was to becoming a monk. This may sound contradictory as from my early adolescence, I had the deepest desire to be a monk and lead a monk's life. I had gone to the Himalayas to live in monasteries. But I was not ready to become a monk with Baba. This would mean I could not get his company continuously since I would have to travel often. I also had a few reservations. I had my strict lifestyle, which was enough for me. I did not see the need to be a monk. One could lead a monk's life without any external display. By changing the dress only, one did not become a monk.

Lahiri Mahasaya had warned his followers, "Do you think by changing the dress and keeping long hair and beard you will be a monk? Do you think that by giving up the sacred thread and wearing the *rudraksha* (Rosary) you will be a monk? Do you think by putting on a colored mark on the forehead, or smearing ashes you will be a monk? Do not think in this way. If by changing one's outward appearance, by putting on ochre color dress one will be a monk, then all the cows that have ochre color, all the dogs that have ochre color, all the horses that have a reddish shade will be monks. Do not show yourself to be a monk, rather change your life first. Transform your life, then become a monk." I was impressed with these teachings about changing one's inner life. I was not willing to be a monk, and I did not want to come to the West. Yet coming to the West happened in a very dramatic way. Baba literally pressed me to get a passport. He repeatedly asked me if I had already applied for it. To delay the process, I applied for my passport to visit foreign countries as a gazetted officer of the Government of Orissa, Department of Higher Education. I knew that if I applied as a government official, it would take a long time to get clearance from all the different departments. The process was considerably delayed. When I finally got the passport it was valid only for a few countries like the United States, Switzerland, Germany and Saudi Arabia but not applicable to the rest of the world. I kept the passport, but I did not tell Baba that I had it in my possession.

Baba's Play

In the beginning of April 1994, I went to Calcutta for a ten-day vacation, to spend time with Gurudev and meditate. During this time I stayed in the house of a disciple and every morning my host would bring me to Debi Baba's house, where Gurudev was staying. From morning until nighttime, for around twelve hours, I would be with Gurudev, meditating and serving him in whatever he needed. Two days after my arrival, in the evening, Baba suddenly turned to me and said, "I am very happy that you have come here, you stayed with me for a few days. Please go back to Cuttack." He hugged me and blessed me. I was astonished, as far as my memory could stretch, any time I had come to see Shri Gurudev, he had always encouraged me to extend my stay. In the past I had taken an additional two or three weeks' leave from work just to be with him. I felt very disappointed. As I came downstairs to Debi Baba's office he said to me, "Tomorrow, please come in the morning and we will go with Gurudev to register some documents, we want you as a witness." I found it difficult to say yes or no. If I agreed, I would not be able to go back to Cuttack as Baba wanted me to do. If I said no, he would require an explanation. I just looked at him and smiled.

When my host was taking me back to his home, I asked him, "Could you please make arrangements for my return to Cuttack tomorrow?" He was very surprised and asked me if I had an urgent commitment. I explained that it was Gurudev's wish that I should go back the next day. My host and his entire family were very unhappy with the news, they tried to persuade me, "It might be Baba's play with you. You should not go. Even if you do not go to Baba, you can stay with us. At least we will get your company." I spent a restless night. Next morning, my host convinced me to go with him to Debi Baba's house. I came along with some reluctance, still unsure about what to do and sat in Debi Baba's office while my friend went up to talk to Gurudev. I never knew the content of their conversation, but Gurudev telephoned from the third floor and asked me to come up. I felt rather guilty as in a way, I was disregarding the Guru's instructions. When I went up, I bowed down to him, he hugged me and soothingly said, "Are you sad? Don't be sad. I was playing with you. I had no intention of hurting you. Is there any greater gain than the company of the Guru? So stay here and enjoy my company. You come and sit on my bed." In India, a disciple would never sit on the Guru's bed. A Guru is treated with the utmost respect and regard. I sat hesitantly, on the very edge.

Then, in one of those strange moments in life when things change and are never the same, Baba asked me, "Do you hate Western disciples? Do you dislike Western disciples?" I was really sad to hear this. I have never hated anyone in my life. At that time, I was more shy, introverted and silent. I looked at him seriously and said, "No Baba." The all-important question came, "Why don't you come to the West? I have requested you several times to come." I did not reply. I just calmly looked at him. So he pressed me to answer, "Tell me, you will come or not?" It was among the most critical moments in my life. I could not say yes, as I was still unwilling to come to the West, but if I said no it would cause him pain. So I did not say 'yes' or 'no'. Gurudev continued, "Till now I thought you were very simple," he added with a certain humor, "And that you would follow me in every step. But today I know that you are very strong and adamant and you will not follow me." I did not react. I just went on looking at him. He became insistent, "Tell me, yes or no? You will come to the West or not?" Still I did not reply. "Nod your head to say 'yes' or 'no', if you do not want to say it verbally." I did not move. Then he added jokingly, "Do you have pain in your neck? When people get spondulitis, doctors give a belt for the neck so that they cannot move their neck and keep it rigid. Have you become a stiffed-neck person?" I continued to stare silently at him. Finally, he used his famous weapon, "Will you follow your Guru or not?" When this question comes, there can only be one answer. He knew this so to round up the matter he added, "You see, Guru only has the best wishes in mind. The Guru wants the all-round development of the disciple. The Guru wants his disciple to excel him in every respect. The Guru is more than the father and the mother. If the child excels the parents, that is a source of pride to the parents, a great joy. Similarly, if a disciple excels and becomes prominent, it is a source of joy to the Guru. Please follow me and come to the West. Come at least once. I want to show my Western disciples and students that I have a disciple like you." There were tears in my eyes and again I bowed down at his feet. My unwillingness to come to the West, so early in life, disappeared. The direction of my life had changed from one moment to the next.

That same day, we went to register some documents. As I sat beside Gurudev in the back seat of the car, he talked on happily about life in the West, and on the way, he pointed out the location of the German Consulate, the Austrian Consulate, the Swiss Consulate and explained to me how to get a visa. I was only half listening, having reverted to a state of apprehension at being put in such a situation when I did not want to come to the West before the age of fifty. When we came back, he started asking me several questions, "I know that you always take vegetarian food, but if somebody takes non-vegetarian food next to you, will you be unhappy? Orthodox religious people are very particular about their food habits and style". I was wondering why he was asking me this question. But I replied, "No. Why should I be unhappy with other people's food? If somebody is taking food, let him eat his food with love. I will eat my food and I will be happy with it. Food is for our spiritual progress. We should not hate any food. In the Upanishads it is written; *Annam na nindyat* - never blame food at all. *Annam brahma iti vyajanat* - know that food is the manifestation of God's power and God's love. So I don't blame anybody's food." But he wanted a more specific answer, "Can you take food with somebody who is taking non-vegetarian food sitting next to you?" I answered, "It will create no problem for me." Still unsatisfied he persisted, "If somebody is taking non-vegetarian food and by mistake some part falls on your plate, what will you do? Will you throw the food away, or you will not eat that part of it?" He was trying to judge my tolerance. I said, "I will not throw the food. I would never waste food. I will not eat the non-vegetarian food, I would take the vegetarian food with love." Finally he was satisfied. He assured me that he wanted to bring me to Europe first and then to the United States. He also elaborated about my destiny and future.

I went back to Cuttack and my college with a heavy heart as I was not mentally happy about going to the West so early in life. One Saturday evening, while I was visiting a temple, Gurudev telephoned to the Ashram and asked to speak to me. When I came back around 8 o'clock, the ashramites informed me that Gurudev wanted me to call him back. But the Ashram telephone had no facility for long distance calls. I went to a nearby public telephone office and called Shri Gurudev. Usually Baba rarely picks up the telephone but this time he did. As he talked I kept uttering "Baba, Baba, Baba." Whenever I talk to Gurudev, instead of saying "yes" I always say "Baba." I also address him in the third person, "How is Baba?" instead of the more familiar "How are you?" After watching me for sometime, the telephone operator thought I was a little bit crazy and made big gestures about how big the telephone bill was going to be. I did my best to signal him to stop. Gurudev talked to me for nearly fourty-five minutes, instructing me on the measures I should take for a leave of absence from my teaching job, and telling me to seek my parents' permission to come to the West. I bowed down to Baba over the telephone and Baba blessed me.

In this critical period, Gurudev kept in close contact, sometimes ringing around midnight. He had planned to take me along with him to Europe, but as there was a special program near Zurich, an International Kriya Yoga Seminar, Christine Ma, his disciple from Vienna, had already come to fetch him. Baba explained that he would send me all the sponsorship letters and necessary documents from Europe, in order to fulfill all the visa requirements. He entreated me to follow him faithfully, as quickly as possible. A few days later he left for Europe.

The Departure

I was in the habit of writing to Gurudev every week, whether he replied or not, but during this period I was unable to write. From Europe, Gurudev went to America for a short visit, and his birthday was celebrated in Chicago that year. When he returned to Europe, he was concerned about not getting any correspondence from me. He could feel I was not happy about coming to the West. He therefore wrote several letters, and posted them to all my possible addresses. He also urged some prominent disciples to make sure that I would receive his letters, and follow his instructions. The letters were full of encouragement to join him in the West.

Meanwhile, the sponsorship letters arrived. The first one came from Vienna, sent by Christine Ma and the next one from Holland, sent by Peter Baba, Gurudev's long-time disciple and *yogacharya*. A third sponsorship came from Germany. It was sent by a Pastor from an Evangelic Church, Mr. Wolf Heyman, who was the center leader of

Hamburg at that time. There was no way out. I applied for leave from my job for three months. The necessary changes were made in my passport. I went to Delhi, to get my visas. I got the visa for Austria and for Holland, but not for Germany. I returned to Cuttack to make further preparations before I left. I talked endlessly with Shrimanta Baba, a fellow *brahmachari* and a good and faithful disciple, who was living with me in the recently inaugurated Cuttack Ashram. We worked out a detailed plan for the fledgling Ashram I was leaving behind. Then we both left for Calcutta. During the train journey, I was really concerned about the future, what would happen to the new Ashram if I did not return after the scheduled three months? Shrimanta Baba was a real friend and I will never forget his encouraging words, "You are in a battlefield like a brave warrior. The warrior does not look back. He always looks forward and proceeds. Do not look back. You are going to make history." To reassure me he added, "Do not worry about the Ashram. The effort we made together to construct this Ashram will not go to waste. I will take all possible steps to realize our dream." Till now I cherish these words in my heart as I value his encouragement and loyalty.

Once we reached Calcutta, we purchased some things. Gurudev had given me clear instructions about the orange color clothing I was to use as a *brahmachari* living in the West. *Brahmacharis* should wear white, yellow or orange. Gurudev specifically suggested that I start dressing in orange clothes. It was October 2nd 1994, the com-memoration of the birthday of Mahatma Gandhi, whom I deeply loved and admired. On the day of my departure to Vienna, many international flights were cancelled due to an epidemic that had broken out, resulting in the death of hundreds of people. I was informed by British Airways that my flight was not cancelled, but that I should reach the airport three hours in advance, so that a medical check up could be performed on every passenger. I was staying at the house of Debi Baba, giving me his blessing, the rest of us set out for the airport. Accompanying me were Shrimanta Baba, Bimal Baba, Dr. Ojha Baba and Satya Baba, all beloved disciples of Shri Gurudev.

That day in October 1994, was the most painful day in my life because I was leaving India. I love India with all my heart. India is my place of pilgrimage. India is the holy place that has taught me all the spiritual truths that I know. India is the sacred place that has given me the company of so many great souls in my life. India is the place which has shown me the beautiful way of perceiving divine love within. India is the playground of my childhood, the dreamland of my youth and the most sacred place of pilgrimage for me. The snowy peaks of the Himalayas and the river *Ganga* thrill my mind and heart until now. I was leaving behind holy India, which used to be called Bharat, or the Land of Illumination. No words can express how sad I really felt.

After the medical checkup, I was asked to go inside and was not allowed to go out again. I could only look through the glass pane at my beloved friends. They looked back at me. My heart was heavy. On the other hand, I took solace from the thought of being with Gurudev soon.

I did not have any idea how to pass immigration, customs clearance or check or claiming my baggage. Everything was new to me. I was utterly alone, and it was my first flight. I met a couple from Assam, while waiting for the same flight. They befriended me, and helped me in all possible ways. Everything worked out smoothly and I boarded the plane. Just before I stepped on board, I touched the soil of India. I bowed down to India, my motherland. In India, soil is not a land or a territory or a boundary, India is Mother Earth.

The Vedas declare,

mata bhūmi putroham prithivyā

The mother is this earth and we are her children.

Then the plane took off from Calcutta to Delhi, and from Delhi to London. In London I had to change planes and take another flight to Vienna. Along the way, I spent the whole time in deep meditation praying to God, "Oh God! What is your purpose? I had a plan, I thought if I was to come to the West as a teacher, I would come after the age of fifty, not sooner. I had the plan to make the Ashram in Cuttack self-sufficient and more beautiful and vibrant. I had the plan to spend some years in silence and seclusion. Oh God! Now all my plans have been cancelled. I surrender myself to your plan."

Arrival In Vienna

When I reached Vienna, I came out of the airport, after passing through immigration and collecting my bag. Suddenly, I saw so many beautiful faces full of love. They were waiting with flowers and garlands to receive this small child of God, the little child of Gurudev. They all welcomed me saying, "Welcome Baba! Welcome Baba!" They were all happy. I was neither happy nor unhappy. Christine Ma was to drive me to the Ashram. She wanted me to sit in the front. I automatically walked to the left side of the car, but in Austria it was the place for the driver. They all laughed, asking me to drive. I began to smile.

At that time the Ashram was located in the house of a beloved disciple of Shri Gurudev, Dr. Peter Bäurle, in Beheimgasse 44 in Vienna's 17th District. Gurudev was waiting for us. I went upstairs, Gurudev was beaming that he was victorious and I was defeated. This was my second defeat. I touched his feet with extreme devotion. He embraced me warmly and blessed me whole-heartedly. Blessing me to be successful, he added, "I had the wish of showing the people in the West that I had a disciple like you, and now my wish is fulfilled." He smiled contentedly like a loving father. Many disciples from Vienna were there on that first day and we all sat together to have lunch. Baba and me were sitting close to each other. I was unable to eat. I was looking at him, my eyes were full of tears, but I was not crying. After lunch was over, Gurudev instructed me to take some rest. I went to my new room. The room was nicely decorated with flowers and many comfortable things. Another disciple of Gurudev, Brigitte Ma, took care of Gurudev very nicely. She gave me a glass of water and I took a little rest. In the evening, I spent some time with Gurudev. Then, after dinner, Gurudev told me to rest again. I was unable to sleep, I kept hearing a beautiful sound.

In the middle of the night, I got up from sleep. I thought that it was early morning. Looking at my watch, I went to the bathroom and took a shower. While taking a shower, I heard knocking at the door. I quickly got dressed and came out. Baba was really concerned, "Why are you taking a shower in the middle of the night?" I explained, "Baba, it is early in the morning." I had forgotten to change the time of my watch and I was about four and a half hours early. Baba told me not to be a naughty child and to continue sleeping nicely since it was midnight.

The Dreadful Morning

Three or four days passed peacefully in the company of Gurudev. He was training me in every possible way and preparing me for my stay in Europe. On the 7th of October, a Friday morning, while we were about to take breakfast, Baba called Brigitte Ma and asked her to write down a few words to introduce me in the program to be held that evening. She took down his instructions, and then we all sat for breakfast. While taking breakfast Baba suddenly stopped in the middle, and complained that he was not feeling well. He asked Brigitte Ma to contact Christine Ma and make arrangements for him to be taken to the hospital immediately as he was feeling rather sick. I went with Gurudev to his room without finishing my own breakfast. I sat near his bed. He confirmed that he was feeling most unwell. His blood pressure was dropping and the medicines were not helping at all. I was praying to God, "Oh God! Please help Gurudev gain back his health." Then he said quietly the following words, "Look Baba, I had one wish, it was to bring you to the West and my wish is fulfilled. I have nothing more to wish for at my age and I want you to stay here and you will be loved by all. But today is the day of your first program in Vienna and I am going to the hospital. I also want you to know that I am going to leave my body today." What worse news could I hear? I was shocked beyond words and started crying. I was horrified. What was my Guru saying? Was it true? Why would God bring me here to face this dreadful situation, I was really so happy in India. Why did I come to the West? Gurudev continued, "Don't be unhappy. Today I will leave this body but you are my beloved child. You will stay here." He removed his wristwatch and gave it to me saying, "This is a beautiful wrist watch. You will use it all the time." Baba used a colorful, woolen *ruana* from Colombia whenever he was cold. He looked majestic in it. He told me, "This is my *ruana*. You will keep this with you all the time and here is some money just in case." Then he instructed me in detail about what to do and what not to do. I did not stop crying. He said to me, "Please do not cry! People in the West would be so unhappy to see tears in your eyes. Be strong! Go to the bathroom and wash your face." I did as I was told, but could not help thinking that I could control my tears but not my inner sorrow. What was I doing here? Why did I come? When I came back I sat near him. He started talking about the last ceremony to be performed after he left his body and every word he uttered pierced my heart. Inwardly I was crying, but I was controlling the outward show of tears. I gave him ultra red-hot fomentation on his body. He kept looking at my face and said, "Oh! Your face looks beautiful. It is like your mother's face."

Around 5.30 in the afternoon, an ambulance came. They took out Gurudev on a stretcher and when I bowed to him he said to me, "We will meet in the next life." Brigitte Ma was accompanying Baba. I protested and said, "I do not want Baba to be taken to a hospital." She could not understand me. She insisted that a hospital was a nice place with good accommodations, and that Baba would be more comfortable there. They left and I came upstairs and sat down. I never remember feeling more desolate.

In the Ashram remained Jutta Ma, Brigitte Ma's sister and Roland Baba, a young disciple of Gurudev. They were making arrangements to take me to the evening lecture, which would start at 7 o'clock. I sat there with my head bowed down in grief. Suddenly, I remembered that Gurudev had asked me to inform Debi Baba about his illness. This gave me something practical to do. Roland Baba helped me to make the telephone connection and I talked with Debi Baba. I told him about Gurudev's sickness, but I did not repeat Gurudev's words that he was going to leave his body on that day. Debi Baba listened patiently, and then he said to me, "Please contact all the old disciples in Europe and America and tell them about Baba's condition. Please take note of Baba's health every hour and inform me periodically."

At the Ashram they offered me a snack before I went to the lecture, which I declined since I did not feel like eating. On our way to the lecture hall, I realized I had not given any thought to the topic of my talk. There were about forty to fifty people in the hall. It was my first public appearance in the West. I went and sat in front of them, without looking at anybody in particular. I was heart broken and totally unable to talk. Then I transformed myself thinking, "If God has brought me here to talk, I must fulfill His wish." I remembered Jesus praying to his Heavenly Father, 'Oh God! Oh Father! If you want me to drink from this cup, I will drink. Thy will be done.' After this heartfelt prayer, I started my talk. I still do not know what it was I said, only that it lasted a good period of time. I sang a song. After I concluded my talk everybody came to greet me and I could feel their love, yet I remained in my own world. I do not remember what happened to me that day, I only thank God that everybody was happy.

When we came back to the Ashram, we were about to take some food, but I did not feel any hunger. I just sat there like a statue, no one understood the grief I felt inside. Suddenly the telephone rang, somebody answered and brought the receiver to me, "Gurudev would like to speak with you." When I picked up the telephone, I bowed to Baba and my eyes were full of tears. He said to me, "I am so happy! Congratulations!

You talked so nicely. Everybody is thrilled with your talk. Which song did you sing?" He went on with such a light tone that it hardly felt like the voice of a sick person, least of all the voice of a person who was about to leave his body. Towards the end of the conversation he said, "Baba, I did not bring my wristwatch, the one I gave to you, it is on the table. I did not bring the *ruana*. What I said to you before I left, please forget it. It was a play. Tomorrow, after the initiation ceremony in the hall, you will come straight to me, you will see me here and you will bring my wristwatch and *ruana*. I am happy here. Forget what I said to you. It was a dream. And I am happy that you did such a nice job, all alone and for the first time. Everybody was moved with your talk. Everybody is pleased and satisfied. They could feel that Hariharananda was speaking through you." I was speechless. He was my beloved Gurudev, but if this was a play why would a Guru play in this way with his disciples? Until today this is a mystery I have not yet deciphered. Yet nothing would ever be as bad as this again.

My first program continued for three days into the weekend. Baba stayed in the hospital for more than a week. On the 14th of October, the very next weekend, there was another program in Vienna. Baba had not fully recovered and was therefore unable to come. This time there were people from different parts of Europe, from Germany, Holland and Belgium. The house was really full and this program was really beautiful. More than one hundred disciples attended the meditation. There were also many new initiations.

This is how Gurudev brought me to the West and entrusted me to carry out his mission. Towards the end of October, I had to go to the Holland Ashram for a ten days program. In the meantime, Baba talked to disciples in Germany and requested them to arrange for my visa so that I could also go there. I was praying to God to let me go back home, to India. I left for the Holland Ashram on the 24th of October. I was to leave Vienna at 7 o'clock. It was a cold morning. Around 6 o'clock, Baba came to my room and checked if I was dressed warm enough. He asked me to put on some additional clothing. He told us to leave early. I bowed down to him, and he said to me, "Wherever you go, I am with you. I bless you. My blessing and love will always be with you. You will get victory, you will get success." We found on the way heavy traffic and we appreciated Gurudev's foresight. Anneliese Ma, the secretary of the Ashram, gave me a telephone card and some Dutch currency in case of an emergency.

The Holland Ashram was a blissful and tranquil place, impregnated with the character of Peter Baba, and his kindness. This Ashram was inaugurated in August 1993, by Shri Gurudev. I stayed there for ten days. On my way back, I was hoping and praying to God that I would not get a visa for Germany so that I could go back to India as soon as possible. I reached Vienna on the 7th of November. There was a surprise in store for me, however, between Gurudev's strong, persuasive personality and the sincere effort made by Wolf Baba in Hamburg and Gert Baba in Vienna, they managed to get my visa for Germany. This was a really difficult feat, but they got my passport stamped right away.

Baba was pleased, he was secretly making plans to prolong my stay in Europe. He had told me to bring some papers with me; a letter of recommendation from a high police official, and two letters of recommendation from prominent personalities in India together with my birth and health certificates. Once in Vienna, Baba told me to give all my documents to Christine Ma. I knew they must be somehow related to my stay but not that these papers would be the foundation for a new life abroad. A tranquil month passed in the holy company of Gurudev, meditating and discussing the scriptures.

He Went Back to India

On the 11th of December, a public program got underway. Peter Baba came from Holland, so we were all there. I was really happy to be near Gurudev who had postponed his trip to India. The next morning,

Baba suddenly decided that he was going back to India after all. I distinctly remember the 12th of December as another very painful day in my life. When I had come to the West with all my reservations, I had been sustained by the hope that I would be in the company of Gurudev, serving him. In my life I loved my parents and enjoyed their blessings and their care. I loved my brothers and sister. I loved the teachers in my school. I loved my friends and colleagues. I loved and admired many monks and spiritual teachers in India. I had been inspired and guided by them all. I had tried my best to love all and to serve all. But it was my Guruji that I loved most of all, and I knew he loved me. This love was extremely unusual and special. I cannot express it in words, so what I felt now was really painful. Baba was going back to India, and leaving me alone here. Since he insisted on travelling right away, everything was arranged for his flight immediately. In the afternoon he told me not to come to the airport with him. I was sitting in his room packing his bags. I was writing his name with markers on his suitcases so that it would be easier to recognize his bags once he arrived in India. If I went to the airport, I could be with him for a few more hours, but he was worried about the impact this was going to have on me. Fortunately, Peter Baba persuaded Gurudev that there was enough time to see him off and to be punctual for the start of the new program at 7 o'clock in the evening. We went to the airport. Silently, I kept asking God why he had brought me to the West and was leaving me all alone.

Once we arrived at the airport, more than one hundred disciples were waiting to say good-bye to Gurudev, and I saw tears in their eyes for the first time. They felt the same mixture of love and the pain of separation from their teacher, just like I did. This touched my heart and it was a new bond between me and the Western disciples. Baba talked about spirituality and I sat at his feet, taking notes. He hugged and blessed me, then one by one we all bowed down to him. The dreaded moment came. Christine Ma took Baba in his wheel chair, he waved good-bye. Once he had gone inside, everybody made their way back to Vienna, to the program, for evening meditation. I do not know what came over me, tears started rolling down my cheeks like rain, nonstop, continuously. On each side I had a Peter Baba, like two pillars, one was Peter Baba the *yogacharya* from Holland, and on the other side, Dr. Peter Bäurle, Gurudev's devoted disciple. In the Bible it is said that Peter was the name of Simon and that he would be as strong as stone. They both led me back to the car and did their best to console me. But I was unable to listen to them. It was a strange situation for me while in the presence of others. I have never experienced that kind of a state in my life before. For two hours straight, tears flowed out of my eyes like an endless stream. When we came back to the Ashram, Peter Baba asked me if I would rather rest, or come to the program. I needed to recover my calm, quiet and composed nature. I made myself ready. The loving faces of the Western disciples called me silently, my new life began to take shape.

My Prolonged Stay in the West

When I originally came to Europe, I had taken only three months' leave from my job. All my visas would expire at the end of December, 1994. While I visited Germany to conduct some programs with other *yogacharyas*, Shri Gurudev and Christine Ma were quietly planning to keep me in the West longer and longer, eventually acquiring for me resident status in Austria.

I came back after my trip to Germany on the 19th of December, happy that the day of my return to India and seeing Gurudev again was almost upon me. But on the 21st of December, Dr. Peter Bäurle took me from Vienna to Munich to get my Austrian visa extended for another three months. I was aware of all the efforts being made on my behalf and was grateful to the people involved, but inwardly I could not help feeling a certain sadness. I missed India. When I reached Vienna again, I received a telephone message form Shri Gurudev in which he said, "It is my wish that you should stay longer in Vienna. My child, please do not say 'no'. Try to stay longer. Fulfill my wish. This is the divine duty of a disciple." I stayed, following his command, remembering Yoganandaji's submission to his Guruji, "Your wish is my law."

We celebrated Christmas in Vienna. It was a nice ten-day program, held in the Ashram. Since then I have celebrated every Christmas in Austria. Disciples came from Germany and Switzerland as well as Austria. On Christmas Eve, Baba gave us his special blessing over the telephone. He expressed his great joy and delight that I was staying longer in Europe, and predicted that it would be prolonged indefinitely. He also mentioned that I would visit many European countries. Then he asked Hans Peter Baba, the center leader of Zurich, to make all the necessary arrangements for me to travel to Switzerland.

We celebrated Christmas and New Year in an environment filled with devotion, with meditation sessions lasting until midnight. By mid-January I was given resident-status in Austria. Christine Ma made all the arrangements, so I was able to make Austria the center of my activities. In the meantime, I was invited to visit Germany again. I visited many German cities and started to learn this beautiful language. In March, I went to Switzerland, my first program was in Zurich. On the last day of the program, I came down with chickenpox. It was somewhat unusual to get chickenpox at my age, and people generally believe that the older one is to get chickenpox the harder it is to get well. But I got chickenpox on a Sunday and by God's grace I was completely cured by the next Thursday. During this period, some devoted disciples took me to rest in a beautiful farmhouse on the shore of Lake Constance. On Friday, a new program started in St. Gallen. With God's help I was able to complete both programs.

The Brief Home Coming

Finally, Baba allowed me to come back to India. I was so happy. On the 8th of April, 1995, I boarded the plane from Vienna to London and then from London to Calcutta. After my chickenpox, I was really weak.

On the 9th of April, I reached India. The disciples in Calcutta and Cuttack were really sad to see me in such a poor state of health. Most of them advised me not to return to Europe because they felt I had not been looked after properly. I smiled because I knew how much love and care I had received in Europe. Austria in particular would be my new home if not my homeland. As in every step in life, Gurudev had given me particular instructions. He told me to spend my time in Cuttack and to see my parents. I spent sixteen days in India during that trip. Towards the end of my stay I was supposed to join Baba in Calcutta.

My Last Surrender

My return ticket for Vienna was booked on the 26th of April. On the 20th of April I traveled to Calcutta to meet Gurudev. When he saw how weak I had become, he personally took care of my food so that I would regain my health and strength back.

On the 24th of April, 1995, on a Wednesday evening, Baba called me to his room after meditation. We were staying in the house of Bimal Baba. He suddenly turned to me and announced, "Tomorrow I am going to initiate you into the holy monastic order." As I mentioned earlier, I did not want to do three things. Firstly, to become a teacher of Kriya Yoga. Secondly, I did not want to go to the West at a young age. Thirdly, I did not want to be a monk. Yet I was living like a monk. Still I felt there was no need for formal initiation into monk-hood. One could lead the life of a monk inwardly with self-discipline, self-control, spirituality and meditation. I led a very strict and disciplined life. Nevertheless I preferred to live like an ordinary person, with an inward contemplative and meditative outlook. I do not know exactly what happened on that day. When Baba said, "Tomorrow I am going to initiate you into the monastic order", I could not say no. I surrendered at his feet. This was my last surrender, my last defeat.

Gurudev asked Bimal Baba to make an exhaustive list of all the things necessary for a monk's initiation. That whole night I spent mostly in meditation. The next morning, two disciples and close friends, whom I have known for a long time, came from Cuttack. One was Shrimanta Baba, who had lived with me in the rented Ashram in Cuttack, and who was instrumental in the construction of the new Cuttack Ashram. When I was in Europe he had taken over its management. The other disciple was Ramachandra Hota, whom I had known since he was ten years old. Both reached Calcutta on the 25th of April, very early in the morning, in order to spend my last day with me as I was leaving for Vienna the very next day. They did not know about my monk's initiation and when they heard that I was going to be initiated into a monk's life, they were so enthusiastic and thrilled that they both decided to become monks at the same time. I knew both of them, they were well-educated and came from very respectable Brahmin families. They also happened to be the eldest sons, which usually is an obstacle. They approached Shri Gurudev and expressed their sincere desire to become monks. To my great surprise, Gurudev accepted.

My mind flew back to a memory a few days before. One evening, while we were in Cuttack, Shrimanta Baba had clearly told me that orange-color clothes were good because they were a natural boundary. It was difficult to be in charge of an Ashram, with normal street clothes. Humorously I asked him, "Do you want to be a monk? Come here. I will make you a monk, I will give you orange-color clothes." Of course this was only a joke, I was not even a monk myself, therefore it was clear that I could not be entitled to initiate someone else. However, I must have had a vague premonition because I remember saying to him, "Before you come to Calcutta to see me, go to your parents, have food with them and come back." There is a long standing tradition that when one wants to be a monk, one should go home and have a meal with one's parents, then one should turn back. I had myself done this while I was staying in Cuttack, but since in my case I was living abroad it had a different connotation.

8. Baba in his travels

9. His unique love

10. Reunited in the West

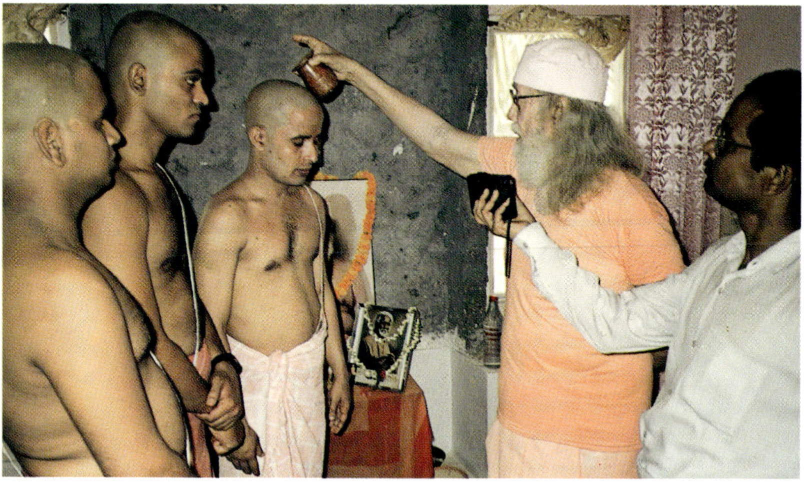
11. Monk's initiation, 25th of April, 1995

12. The second departure to the West, 26th of April, 1995

The Metamorphosis

The 25th of April 1995, was a fundamental turning point in my life. To make it even more significant it fell on a Thursday. Thursday in Sanskrit is called *guruvara* or the day of the Guru, a particularly auspicious day to worship my Guru and his lineage of Masters. On the day of our initiation into the holy monastic order, we renounced the sacred thread and offered it into the holy fire. This is a symbolic burning of the body into the fire, the burning of all worldly desires. We shaved our heads leaving all formal attachments. Gurudev poured holy water on our heads and washed our feet while performing the *abhisheka,* or anointment. The monk's initiation is the day of anointment. In the Bible, it is mentioned that Jesus himself was anointed.

Baba turned to me and said, "Your name is Prajnanananda" (which means 'bliss of wisdom'). To my friend Shrimanta he said, "Your name is Swaroopananda" (which means 'bliss of oneself'). Then he looked intensely at Ramachandra. That day marked the first physical encounter of Gurudev with him. He said, "Your name is Shuddhananda" (which means 'bliss of purity'). We bowed down at his feet. After our monk's initiation, tradition says that new monks should go and beg and also visit a temple. The three of us, accompanied by Bimal Baba, went to the famous Temple of Mother Kali. We prayed earnestly and meditated deeply on this crucial step we had taken in our lives. I remember praying for strength and love in my new monastic path. We went to beg in the neighborhood of Bimal Baba's house, and I remember a very spiritual mother who washed our feet, bowed down to us and then offered us some uncooked rice, some vegetables, some money and finally some sweets. It was a very moving and beautiful day. When we returned we bowed to Gurudev and offered him what we had managed to collect through begging. The rest of the night we spent in prayer and meditation.

The very next day I was to leave Calcutta and return to Vienna. Before I left, I went to court to legally declare that I had been initiated into the monastic order, and that my name was no longer Triloki Dash but Swami

Prajnanananda Giri. From that time onwards, I became 'Prajnanananda'. That whole day, one thought preyed heavily on my mind. I had taken my monk's initiation and it would not be a surprise to anybody. However, the families of my two friends did not know that they had become monks. What made matters worse is that they were each the eldest son of their respective family. No prior notice had been given. What would happen to these families? Parents wish their children success, especially in the material world. Very few are so withdrawn from worldly pressures that they would prefer that their children progress spiritually and reach a higher state of realization. Had I influenced them and motivated them to become monks? As I bid farewell to Gurudev, he blessed me with many things, and reading my mind tried to reassure me with regard to my friends, "Baba, don't be worried about Cuttack. Don't be worried about the new young monks. Everything will be all right. Go with peace of mind." Putting my trust in Gurudev, I felt better. With so much that had changed so quickly, I left India again to head for the West. I had a clearer vision of what lay in store for me in the future.

As soon as I reached Vienna, I wrote two separate letters to the parents of my fellow monks. I narrated the series of events that had led to such a momentous decision and implored them to have patience and strength. A month later I got a reply from both families, which curiously enough arrived on the same day. The letters themselves were similar. Both groups of parents had fully accepted the new path their sons had taken, and they requested me to be always with them as their elder brother. I felt a surge of admiration for these parents, for their strength and understanding. In 1996, when Gurudev went back to Cuttack, both families came and took initiation. Gurudev himself was immensely moved and welcomed them with open arms.

CHAPTER FIVE

My New Life

One is a true lover of God, whose mind is always saturated with love, speaks sweetly, ready to serve, free from hypocrisy, always in a balanced state, polite in behavior, ready to learn, expert in scriptures, full of inner beauty and always cheerful.

Chanakya Neeti

The play of God; the play of Guru is mysterious. It is very difficult to understand what they really want and how they work. Life was changing quickly. Inwardly, I was prepared to face whatever new experiences life would offer, with calm detachment. I would do good and love all.

During my two weeks' trip to India, the disciples of Vienna had moved to a new place, another Ashram and I did not have the address. My plane had been delayed for hours in Delhi. As was my custom I would never take food when I traveled and very late I reached London. In addition, I had no money and no telephone number. I did not know what to do, but I surrendered myself wholeheartedly to God, surely He would take care of me.

I was so delayed I had lost hope of finding any disciples in the airport. But as I came out, I saw a familiar face standing at one side. Relief flooded into me. When I passed the gate, my heart filled with joy as I saw many other disciples. They stood with a banner that read, "WELCOME SWAMIJI", and on each side they decorated it with the flag of Austria and the flag of India. My new life was encompassed in these three symbols. I was really amazed! How could they know? I felt so warmed by their love. This moment stands out in my memory. It marks the start of a new home in another country. I came to stay. I had found my call. God and Gurus had pointed the way, now it was up to me to get the work done.

His Vision of Balighai

In December 1995, Baba called me early one morning to tell me about a dream. In his dream Shriyukteshwarji had directed Gurudev to transfer the property of Balighai to my name. The prediction was that this property should become a beautiful Ashram in the future, a place of international reputation. Many people would come to stay and meditate. I was amazed at the precision of his words. Balighai is eight miles from Puri, close to the sea and is indeed a very beautiful place, an ideal spot to lead an uplifting spiritual life. At the same time I was aware that the property was controversial to some extent. Such is the beauty and potential of this place that some people would be tempted to do a lucrative business transaction instead. In no way did I wish to be mixed up in such things, and spoke seriously and measurably against it. Baba, however, did not take my arguments seriously and in March of 1996, while he was in India and during my absence, he transferred the property to my name. Ever since, he has insisted that his dream will come true through me. As the years pass, Balighai has flourished to become a center of spirituality. Once more I see in my mind's eye the long-range vision and wisdom of Gurudev.

My first Attempts to be an Author

From my childhood I loved books. It would really fascinate me how people would get the inspiration to write books. It was my belief that people who wrote books were gifted by God. During my school and college days, I was always involved in writing articles and publishing journals, but I never dreamt of becoming an author.

When I was teaching Economics, a long time friend of mine came to me and requested me to write a small book on the life of Swami Vivekananda, which he wanted to print and publish. I was hesitant, but he convinced me that I was the right person for the job. I wrote this book in Oriya and it was published in 1993, to commemorate the centenary of Swami Vivekananda's address in the historic Parliament of World Religions, held in Chicago.

From December 1994 until March 1995, I was alone in Germany and Switzerland while conducting some programs. During these four months I felt a deep connection with Shri Gurudev, so I noted down every thought that came to me about his teachings. Two small volumes were born out of this attempt, 'Words of Wisdom' and 'Nectar Drops'. Brigitte Ma took some notes and Andreas Baba, a dedicated disciple from Hamburg, typed the manuscripts. We got them printed in the beginning of 1996. During my stay in the West, Baba constantly encouraged me by saying, "Please write something. Everyday you should write for at least forty-five minutes. You should not waste time. You know all the scriptures and their inner meanings, you should write." On Guru Purnima day in 1995, he was particularly insistent, "I have one request for you, be my instrument. You are explaining the Holy Bible in such a nice way, in the same way I have taught you. Please write a book on the Holy Bible, with its metaphorical interpretation, correlating it with the Indian Scriptures". When I heard this, the memory of the conversation between Babaji and Shriyukteshwar at the *Kumbha Mela* in Allahabad came to my mind. I bowed down to him and said, "If Gurudev gives me his blessings, everything is possible." Within four months, starting from that Guru Purnima in the month of July until the month of November, I completed his request. The book was titled, 'The Torah, The Bible and Kriya Yoga.' My hand-written notes were typed by Ulrich Baba, who was a sincere disciple of Gurudev for nearly twenty years. During Gurudev's birthday in 1996, this book was presented to him.

Another crucial incident occurred that same year. It was the special occasion of *Nava Kalevara* or the renewal of the images of the three deities in the Temple of Jagannath. Gurudev got a letter from the Temple Authority to write an article to commemorate this important festivity. The renewal of the deities is an auspicious occasion in both the Hindu tradition and the Jagannath culture. Baba asked me to write an article based on some suggestions. I elaborated on his notes, which eventually became a book of more than one hundred pages. It was written in Oriya.

When I showed Baba the result of my work, he was very enthusiastic and advised me to get the book printed in India. Through Gurudev's inspiration, I was able to give a yogic interpretation of all the activities related to Lord Jagannath's shrine.

When the first volume of 'The Bhagavad Gita' was printed, I said to Baba, "Gurudev, the Bhagavad Gita consists of eighteen chapters, therefore this work with its metaphorical interpretation in the light of Kriya Yoga should be completed." Gurudev argued that he was getting older and his health was not as good. I humbly suggested that he should give me some notes and dictation. In this way, with my Guru's grace and God's blessings, the work was finished. The remaining twelve chapters of the Bhagavad Gita, with a metaphorical interpretation were printed in two volumes during 1998 and 1999. They made a wonderful birthday gift for Gurudev.

My Master has always been my source of inspiration and as I undertake every new work my mind and memory turn to him and to his teachings. It is his ideas that flow through my pen in a subtle way.

The First Visit to America

Gurudev had expressed his desire to bring me to America. Several attempts were made to arrange for my visa. I myself was not quite prepared so that when it proved difficult to get the visa, I was not disturbed in the slightest. But ultimately the strong will of the realized Master is successful. Through the strong determination of my Guruji, and the efforts of Don Baba, I finally obtained my visa for America. The same consular officer in Calcutta, who had previously refused my visa application, after gathering supplementary documentation, reversed her decision. The letter reached the Cuttack Ashram and was forwarded to Europe. I got my visa for the USA and on the 23rd of April, 1996, I came to America for the first time to attend a Kriya Yoga International Seminar, in New York. Shri Gurudev was extremely pleased, and predicted that I would also travel to South America, Australia, Japan, China and Russia.

The Materialization of a Dream

The construction of the new Ashram in Cuttack began in January 1993 and was completed in May. Unfortunately Gurudev was not in Puri or in Cuttack, to bless and purify this Ashram with his holy presence. In 1994, I myself went to the West. In 1996, I came back to India for nearly two months. During this period, I spent most of my time in Cuttack. I requested Gurudev to come to the Ashram while I was there, but due to his many commitments he was unable to come. Once again I had to return to the West. While I was in Europe, one night I had a dream that I was back in the Cuttack Ashram and found Gurudev there. I bowed down at his feet and offered him a flower garland.

Sometime later and to my astonishment, I had to return to India again in the month of March, for a short period of time, to attend the annual celebration of the Puri Ashram on the 21st of March. I flew from Belgium to London and then to Calcutta. That was on the 17th of March. On the same evening, Gurudev was supposed to reach Puri. It was a pity because Baba would be in the same area, but I would miss him by a day. I was a little disappointed that my dream would not come true, that I would not have the chance of seeing Gurudev in Cuttack. However, while I was in Calcutta I learnt that Gurudev had postponed his trip for one day and would be in Cuttack at the same time. My joy knew no bounds. In the evening I boarded the train to Cuttack, and very early I reached the Cuttack Ashram. The Ashram was full of flowers. And Gurudev was looking through the window as I entered. The disciples were blowing the conch and everybody was full of joy, peace and happiness filled with the holy presence of Gurudev. I bowed down at his feet, offering a flower garland. This was the materialization of my dream. What I had seen in my dream came true by the grace of God and Gurus.

Gurudev and the Jagannath Temple

It is a rare chance to visit a holy place in the physical company of one's own spiritual guide. To go to the Jagannath Temple with Gurudev is a beautiful memory. In Sanskrit there is a proverb, '*Guru-Govinda-Darshana*', Guru is the Master, Govinda means God, *darshana* is to have a vision. Inside the Temple, people have the vision of God in one of His manifested forms. But the Guru helps us to have the vision of God in our body temple.

As was our tradition, every year we set out on foot from the Karar Ashram to the Jagannath Temple. While Gurudev sat on a *rikshaw,* the disciples would travel by foot, singing the name of God. We would all be singing and chanting in chorus accompanied by musical instruments. In 1986, when we were at the steps leading to the Temple, a priest came out and he rudely addressed Gurudev because he spent so much time in the West. We all witnessed the humility of Gurudev, who, without reacting to such rudeness did his best to pacify the priest. Just at that moment, the chief priest of the Temple came with a big flower garland, belonging to the deity, and put it around Gurudev. The other priest, rather ashamed, left in silence. We were all gratified that Lord Jagannath had sent his own priest to receive Baba with due honor. That same evening, the District Magistrate and Police Officials came to the Ashram, and having heard of the incident in the Temple, were very apologetic. Gurudev full of love and humility explained that human life was full of extremes, therefore we should learn to maintain the state of equanimity.

The Jagannath Temple is famous for religious festivals and celebrations. Many times on the occasion of the Car Festival, I had the rare opportunity to go with Shri Gurudev and have the vision of the three deities, Jagannath, Balabhadra and Subhadra, on their three beautifully decorated chariots. Gurudev with folded hands, full of devotion, would be praying to God. In the scriptures it is said,

rathetu vāmanam drushtvā punarjanma na vidyate

Ratha means chariot, which is large in size. The deity inside the chariot looks small. So *vamana* means dwarf. This means that having seen God in the miniature form, inside the chariot, one will not be reborn and will be able to reach liberation. Symbolically this body is a chariot, with the senses as horses, pulling in different directions. In this body chariot, God is hiding in a miniature form, in the cave of the cranium and one who experiences the Soul in every breath, will find liberation. In this way, my Master, holding my hand as the chariot passed, explained how to experience God within. Around us would be assembled more than half a million people in order to get a glimpse of God, in one of His forms, on this rare occasion once in a year. Looking at the mass of devotees with their eyes transfixed on the deities in the chariot, Gurudev would turn to me and say, "This is *ananta atma pravaha,* meaning the flow of infinite souls. It is the river of life and love." Everyone's eyes were focused with reverence towards their image of God.

When we entered into the Temple, Gurudev would bend down his head, kneeling and touching the stepping stone, and taking a little dust or sand, would put it on his forehead. He would instruct me, "Take the dust, and put it on your forehead. This is not ordinary dust. This is the dust from the feet of millions of devotees who visit here with hearts overflowing with love and devotion. They come to Puri because they are overwhelmed with troubles and difficulties, to get the *darshan* of Lord Jagannath. Their love and their devotion have sanctified the sand. Put it on your forehead. Be pure and feel the same love as you enter this holy shrine." Gurudev is always merged in the state of unity, or *advaita bhava*, yet he never hesitates to manifest his devotion and love.

The full moon in the month of June is known as *snana purnima*, on this day the deities in the Temple are brought out, placed on the open altar and given a ceremonial bath. The three deities are beautifully decorated. During this festival, thousands of pilgrims congregate to offer their love and devotion to their beloved Lord. People generally stand in front of the Temple, on the main road so that they could have a clear view. Gurudev and me, in order to avoid the crowd, would be standing a little further on the road, this allowed us to have a silent vision of the three deities. Gurudev never missed an opportunity to teach me how to love God.

Once we were already living in the West, Gurudev would look back on those days in Puri with a certain nostalgia. He would say to me, "How grateful I am to Lord Jagannath that He allowed me to be in Puri for such a long period of time. I came to Puri for a few months to stay in the Karar Ashram, and to meditate in seclusion. Lord Jagannath and Shriyukteshwarji allowed me to stay for years and years continuously. I stayed from 1936 until 1974. Thereafter, although I have been living in the West, I have come back many times to this Temple, in the holy city of Puri. I am grateful to Lord Jagannath. I am grateful to Shriyukteshwarji. I am grateful to the vast ocean full of majestic glory. As the three deities in the Temple, to me the ocean, Shriyukteshwarji and Lord Jagannath are three vital aspects in my life."

Gurudev explained what the three deities symbolized for him: Jagannath was God living inside the Temple, Subhadra or the manifestation of knowledge, was like Shriyukteshwarji in the Karar Ashram, Balabhadra or the vastness of God was reflected in the ocean, full of glory, majesty, strength and beauty. When one enters the Jagannath Temple, on the left side lies Balabhadra, in the center is Subhadra and on the right side stands Jagannath. Likewise, Gurudev maintained that in the left side lies the ocean, in the middle stands the Karar Ashram of Shriyukteshwarji, and on the right side rises the Jagannath Temple.

This is true even if one stands on the Karar Ashram's roof, on the left side one can see the vast ocean, the marvelous beauty of God, directly ahead lies Shriyukteshwar's Temple, and if one looks towards the right, in the far distance, one can see the top of the Jagannath Temple, with its flags waving and hurling in the wind.

As the years went by, Gurudev was conscious that his health had somewhat diminished and his body had become weaker. He could not walk around as easily, much less climb steps. On the 18th of March, 1996, we reached Puri. One day later, in the company of some of his Swamis and disciples we arrived at the Jagannath Temple. Gurudev stood in front of the Temple filled with overpowering love in his heart and tears in his eyes. He wondered if God would give him the opportunity once more to go inside the Temple, the strength to climb the steps. He vividly demonstrated the power of a Yogi. Although he looked frail, Gurudev entered the Temple. On each side, two Swamis helped him and as Gurudev climbed up slowly, he entered each Temple and bowed down with devotion, offering his love. We sat for a good period of time in different parts of the Temple court and meditated silently. At the end Gurudev told us to bring some *prasad*, or holy food offered to the deities from the Ananda Bazaar or the market of bliss. Gurudev put some in his mouth and fed us the rest. This was a chance to distribute bliss to us.

Love and Service

Gurudev is the symbol of service. He knows two things: to love and to serve. During the celebration of the Puri Ashram's Foundation Day, there is a meaningful example of his service to others. The whole day there was a huge crowd, composed of hundreds of devotees who visited the Ashram, and came to the meditation room, the Temple of Shriyukteshwar, and even to Baba's room. At nighttime people would rest in various places inside the meditation hall, outside in the hall, under the trees, everywhere. During the night, Gurudev would go around to see if everyone was well, and would give his love silently to everybody, appreciating the pain and discomfort involved in coming such a long way to stay in the Ashram, just to see him and to meditate in his presence. One night, he saw a disciple trembling due to cold and fever. He did not have sufficient clothes to keep himself warm. Gurudev went back to his room to get his woolen shawl, and gently wrapped it around the body of the disciple, who slept on beautifully for the rest of the night. I was a witness. After going round the Ashram, Gurudev finally took rest. The next morning when the disciple woke up, he saw the beautiful shawl covering his body. He recognized Gurudev's shawl. He was greatly moved by the compassion of his Guru. In the morning, he bowed down to Gurudev, thanked him for his love and returned the shawl. Gurudev said, "No! Keep it as a token of my love for you. Remember all the time that it is not a shawl wrapped around your body, it is the love of the Guru which is wrapped around you, so remain all the time in Guru-consciousness, change your life and be divine." This lesson of love, compassion and faith was meant for all those who witnessed this moving episode.

A Touch of Wit

One day I was with Shri Gurudev and we went to visit the Superintendent of Police in Puri, to discuss some problems we were facing in the Ashram. When Gurudev entered his residence, the police officer came with devotion, touched the feet of Baba and knelt down to seek his blessing. In the course of the conversation, the police officer commented that Gurudev was not a good judge of people as he was too loving and thought everyone was good. He reminded Gurudev of an incident far back when he had informed Baba that a certain person was not of good character but Gurudev had insisted that he was good, almost like a son to him. In worldly terms, Gurudev was proved wrong, as the person in question became more and more disreputable as time passed. With the vanity of a police officer, the high official kept asking, "Tell me Baba. Whose judgment was correct? Your judgment or my judgment? I told you he was bad eight years ago." I noticed that Gurudev remained totally indifferent and kept looking at the police officer with a smile. Then he answered with a story, "Two men were taking a bath in the holy *Ganga.* One was a monk and the other was a thief. It was really very early in the morning. The monk, looking at the thief, thought how spiritual the man was, coming so early in the morning and taking a bath in the *Ganga.* The thief looking at the monk thought he might be a thief like him. He had just finished his nightly raid and had come to refresh himself, before he rested during the day. In his mind he was already calculating that with an extra thief to help him along, business could multiply. With these thoughts in mind, the thief approached the monk, 'My dear friend, how are you? How is business? Are you getting something?' The thief was using code language to learn how profitable stealing was in the area. The monk looked at the thief with tears in his eyes, and said, 'Since long I have been following all the instructions of my Guru. I am practicing all the techniques that he taught me, but till now I have not achieved the ultimate goal. My friend, have you been able to get the vision of God?' The monk was looking at the thief and seeing a monk in him. And the thief while looking at the monk had seen a thief in him. The thief was startled from his reverie, 'Oh God! He is not a thief, he is a monk.' Then he took a deeper look at the monk and said, 'My friend, you follow your Guru and you will surely reach your goal. I am following my Guru and whatever I get I am happy. You should not follow me or my Guru. I should not follow you or your Guru'."

With this symbolic story Baba indicated that he only sees the good in all. So to see good in all is the quality of a true monk. He is a divine person not a police officer. I was happy to hear this reply from Gurudev and see the smile in the face of the police officer, who took the lesson well. There was both love and trust between them.

At another time, this high official told me before I left for Europe, "When you see Gurudev, bow down to him for me and request him to bless me and my family. I will tell you one thing, in my life I have seen many monks and visited many Ashrams. I have seen one real monk and he is your Gurudev Baba Hariharanandaji. Please convey my regards and respect to him." The strong link between Baba and his disciples never ceased to amaze me.

CHAPTER SIX

Divinity Manifested through Renuncitation

Where there is charity and wisdom, there is neither fear nor ignorance.
Where there is patience and humility, there is neither anger nor disturbance.
Where there is poverty and joy, there is neither covetousness nor avarice.
Where there is inner peace and meditation, there is neither anxiousness nor dissipation.

St. Francis of Assisi

One day as Gurudev and I were traveling through Orissa, we saw a monk who was nearly 126 years old. His name was Vishwanath Baba. He belonged to an order of monks called *Alekh Sampradaya*. They believe in a formless God, and do not worship any deity. These monks travel only on foot and when they become very old, they are taken in a hand-drawn *rickshaw*, pulled by a devotee. When we happened to pass the *rickshaw* in which this monk was traveling, Baba could not stop the car, but from his seat he folded his hands and bowed down with devotion and high regard. He took this opportunity to teach me that by sharing the company of a holy man, a person would be inspired by the virtue of non-attachment or *vairagya*, love for God and a spirit of renunciation. A dedicated monk was the true ideal of renunciation, therefore a person who had lived such a long life as a monk was really truly remarkable. He quoted,

"sādhunām darśanam punyam"

To be in the presence of an enlightened person helps to transform our mind. It is even more uplifting to sit near them and to listen to their teaching. Most fortunate are those who can serve them physically.

Guru as the Mother

Gurudev is like a mother, he loves and guides his disciples like children. In April 1995, when I was still recovering from chickenpox, Baba nursed me with tender care. One day, early in the morning, while I was meditating in my room, Baba called me. When I went to his room, he asked me to sit down on his chair and eat the food that was on his table. I hesitated to sit on his chair, and wanted to sit on the floor at his feet. Usually it is a tradition that disciples never use, out of deep respect, any material object destined for the use of the Guru. But he held my hand and said, "Sit down! You are sitting on my lap." This is the love of Guru. He assured me, "You and me are one, there is no difference." He made sure I ate everything to recover my strength and vitality.

My Guruji has also been a permanent source of inspiration. My best meditation has always been to be near him, to look at him. When I look at him, my mind automatically gets introverted and floats in the plane of super-consciousness. I feel so much of joy, so much love. He always directed me to keep my attention on the top of my head, or near the occipital bone, and to concentrate there and feel God's presence in every breath. To be with Baba is a meditation in itself, and it is really an enjoyable opportunity to remain constantly and continuously in God-consciousness. I bow to God and Gurus for having given me such a Master, such a caring teacher.

Whenever I went on prolonged errands, Gurudev as a mother, would quickly measure my condition and make sure I ate and rested. Once we were visiting an Ashram, which had an acute food shortage. In the morning there was no food available. We managed to give some breakfast to Gurudev. Gurudev knew this and kept asking me, "Have you taken some breakfast?" I answered, "Yes." Then he pressed me, "What breakfast have you taken?" Since I had had a small ripe banana, I said, "I have taken banana." Gurudev laughed and replied, "Do you know what is the meaning of taking banana in Bengali?" I was surprised, so he continued, "You have taken nothing." He then instructed me to open his bag and take some biscuits to eat. He would reprimand me, arguing that food was necessary for a healthy body and that without proper food how could I serve him. Gurudev, as a mother, would also go around the Ashram, making sure everyone was fine. He would look attentively at every detail and silently continue. Often he would be interested in what I was reading, and would ask me to read out whole passages aloud. Even during the night, after everybody had gone to bed, he would come out with a flashlight in his hand and he would tour the Ashram inspecting everything. He would keep a caring, watchful eye on everyone, all the time.

Gurudev, a Master of Many Languages

Gurudev was adept at speaking many languages. He was born in Bengal, but lived a major part of his life in Orissa. He also spoke Hindi and Sanskrit. When he came to the West, he had both the inclination and a good ear to pick up languages. His cosmopolitan outlook and his love for all nationalities became a great source of inspiration for me.

By the grace of God, I knew Bengali from my childhood. Nobody actually taught me, I learnt it by myself. My family spoke in Oriya. Later on through more formal studies and practice I was able to speak and sing in Bengali fluently. This was good because Gurudev is a beautiful singer, he can sing songs in many different languages. His favorite songs are from the writings of Rabindranath Tagore, the great Bengali poet. I was also familiar with many of these songs. Baba encouraged me to sing not only in Bengali but also in Oriya and Hindi, teaching me how to sing with proper rhythm.

Gurudev also trained me in English. Although I had studied in this language, he directed me to speak more slowly and clearly. Previously, I had had the habit of speaking very fast. He would always insist that I should make proper pauses so that I could be better understood. He also told me to use short and simple sentences, which would clearly portray what I was trying to express.

As I look back, it becomes obvious that ever since my earliest acquaintance with Gurudev, while I was still in my twenties he was grooming me to speak clearly and coherently, preparing me for a more public role.

When I stayed for a few months in Vienna, listening to German so often, I started to speak slowly. Many disciples encouraged me during my learning process. At a certain point, I was able to guide meditation in German. Gurudev was extremely happy to see this. He was a permanent source of inspiration to learn other languages.

Through his encouragement and appreciation, I delivered talks at different places, in different Indian languages. He would listen to the talks carefully and attentively. If there was a mistake, he would make a note and later on would correct me in a very loving way. He was specially exacting with my English.

His Insight

Many years ago, Gurudev was in the house of one of his beloved disciples, a Justice of the High Court of Orissa, Mr. Lingaraj Rath. At that time Gurudev's nephew, Debi Baba, who was Gurudev's first disciple, was also there. I was sitting in Gurudev's room, taking some notes, when they both came in and requested Baba to go to the living room. Baba did not want to go. They did not tell Baba the reason why they needed him, but after repeated requests he finally agreed. I followed Gurudev and was surprised as everyone else when he sat on the couch facing the wall, with his back to all of us. We were baffled by the play of Gurudev. Why would he behave in such a way? Then Gurudev, in a determined way, gave us a sample of his foresight, "You want to show me a video of the Ramayana?" They were surprised he knew and so they said "yes" quietly. "You want to show me the episode in which Vasistha, Rama's Guru, teaches him how to concentrate in each *chakra* and how to meditate, right?" They were even more amazed. Debi Baba argued that it would be interesting for Gurudev because his teachings were being telecast all over India. Gurudev turned to Debi Baba and to Lingaraj Rath and added, "With your eyes open, you have seen in this body the light in each *chakra*. Having seen this with your eyes open, how long do you meditate and how much have you transformed your lives? If you do not change your life looking at the living Guru, having had the direct experience of seeing light in all his *chakras*, how will some videos and movies help you to change your life?" We were all transfixed. After a while he allowed them to show the episode in the video. When I saw the film, my attention was fixed on my Guru and I was thinking, we have the living Vasistha teaching us how to meditate, but we are not worthy like Rama and Lakshmana to follow his instructions. The omniscient Guru knew beforehand what his disciples were going to do. He sees through his inner eye.

Another curious example of his foreknowledge came when I had the opportunity to read and reply the letters that were sent to him. As usual, wherever Gurudev is, there is a good amount of mail everyday. Many times I have seen how he replies every letter meticulously.

As I became closer to him, he allowed me to open, read and would often dictate a reply. This I do even today, when I stay near him in different Ashrams. Through this process the feelings, experience and devotion of his numerous disciples are clearly visible. Before opening each letter, I would read out the return address to Baba, to make sure that I could go ahead and open it. Before the letter was unfolded, he would describe the text almost word for word. When I started reading, I was amazed again and again to find that the contents of the letter were exactly as he had predicted.

He also took this opportunity to encourage me to reply the letters in different languages. If the letter came from Bengal, he would tell me to write back in Bengali. I acquired plenty of practice in writing in Bengali or Hindi. This lesson served me well, and I apply it to my own correspondence. What really made everyone around him perform their best, was that at the end of the exercise, he would always say something encouraging like how nice my handwriting was, or how pleased he was at my speed.

His Care for Details

There is a small incident, which clearly shows how meticulous Gurudev was. We were in the Karar Ashram, and as Gurudev was going to initiate people in the main hall, I locked his door and kept the key in my pocket. In the middle of initiation, he stood up suddenly and left the place. I followed Gurudev, and he asked me to open his room. Once he was inside, he asked me if I knew the reason why he had left. When I shook my head, he explained, "When you will be Guru, you should be careful of everything, even of your nails. If you see my nails, they are cut very short, but still when I was initiating, my nail scratched a new disciple's ear, so he lost his concentration. I came here to trim my nail."

This is a true quality of a Guru, to look after every detail. He taught me that when you become a spiritual teacher you must be careful about what you say, how you look at others and how you behave in every way.

Gurudev was also very particular about personal appearance and presentation. He often taught his monks and disciples that everybody should be careful of three D's. The first D was dress, the second D was demeanor, the third D was dialogue. Through these three elements a person would be known.

On another occasion, Gurudev pointedly taught me that while giving a public talk, it was best not to look at any person as this would only make him/her body-conscious. It was advisable to look at everybody or to remain in a *shambhavi* state. A Guru always sets himself up as a clear-cut example.

His Punctuality

Gurudev is the symbol of punctuality. In every step of his life he is punctual. He always rises early in the morning and does everything at the proper time. While going to a program he is never late. He trains us to be punctual. When we have a program outside the Ashram, he is often ready before anyone else, waiting for us to fetch him. If anyone is just a few minutes late, he would not hesitate to say, "Why are you so late? Why are you not ready before we start. We should be punctual. If we are teachers, we should be teachers in every aspect of our life." Gurudev also believes that to come before an appointment is not considerate. Once we reached a dentist appointment 10 minutes early. Gurudev said, "We should not go ten minutes early to the dentist. If we go in, he really loves us so his mind will be near us, and he will sometimes come out to see us, to talk to us and not give his full attention to his other patients. It is not good." So we sat in the car, a few yards from the clinic, and waited. We only entered the building at the precise time we were expected. The punctuality of Gurudev is very thorough, not early and not late.

Be My Doctor

After my monk's initiation, when we were back in Europe and staying in Hamburg, a grand function was arranged to celebrate Gurudev's birthday on the 27th of May, 1995. But the night before, Gurudev was feeling unwell and his blood pressure was going down. He took some medicines but there was no improvement. I was wondering what action to take, when Gurudev instructed me to give him an injection to bring his blood pressure up. Till that day I had never given an injection to anyone. I suggested that I should call a doctor disciple, staying close by. But Baba said, "No, you give me the injection." To follow the Guru is not always easy. I took the disposable syringe, prepared it carefully with the medicine, and with some alcohol I sterilized Gurudev's hip. Remembering Guru, thinking of Guru, I gave him the injection. He never felt it. When he asked me why I was taking my time, I told him that he had already had his injection. Gurudev was very happy, "Oh! You were so quick. I could not feel it. You are an expert doctor."

Gurudev tests us in many ways. After a short time his pressure went up. I was lying down on the floor of his room, when he ordered me, "Go to your room and take rest. Now I feel well. You need not be worried."

In my time with Gurudev, I have seen that he is a good doctor, having very thorough knowledge of medicine and health. He is also a mobile dispensary. He carries with him a good amount of medicines. He knows his health and is very accurate regarding other people's needs. He helps and guides people physically, mentally and spiritually. Living with him, one is able to learn in many areas of life.

Gurudev had a longstanding familiarity with medicine. His father was a good homeopath. At that time in India the health care facilities were not so abundant. Community leaders often served people's needs according to their capacity. Gurudev's two brothers were medical doctors, they made outstanding contributions.

Gurudev inherited this serviceful attitude from his family and practiced it throughout his life. His motto became, "Give education to the children, food to the hungry, medicine to the sick and compassion and support to the suffering."

While living in Puri, Gurudev would visit the local hospitals to visit some sick disciples, undergoing some treatment. Many times I had the opportunity to accompany him. It was very moving to see how he would bless these sick patients, showing concern about their pain and discussing their condition with their respective doctors. Sometimes Gurudev would offer his own advice, which was well appreciated. Other times, to promote someone's quick recovery, he would meditate and would additionally ask us to meditate in a group, so that through God's grace, the ailing person would find peace and balance.

Love for All Creatures

Gurudev not only loves his fellow humans, he also loves animals. He has a special love for cows and at each Ashram in India, he carefully supervises the cowshed and looks after the health of each animal. When I was still a student and started living in the Ashram of Bhubaneshwar, I also took care of the cows. Among many other duties I had to clean the cowshed, and feed the cows twice a day. Once in the Karar Ashram, one of the cows was having a very difficult delivery. The veterinarian was delayed. The situation was becoming critical, Gurudev asked me to bring some soap, oil and hot water. After cleaning his hands, he put some oil on them and expertly helped the cow in what was a very complicated delivery. At this point the veterinarian arrived and between them the calf was delivered. The cow was safe, but the calf, due to its traumatic birth, was having difficulty in breathing. The pulse was very low and it was about to die. The veterinarian was helpless. Gurudev told me immediately to go to his room and to bring two medicines; one is a homeopathic medicine, 'Pulsatilla', and the other was 'Decadron', a life-saving injection that increases the pulse, circulation and blood pressure. I hurried away. A human dose was appropriate for a calf also. The doctor was really amazed that Gurudev was so quick-witted to use these two life-saving drugs. He gave the injection to the calf, while Gurudev put some Pulsatilla drops inside the calf's mouth. Within a few minutes the calf regained its strength and stood up and started sucking milk from its mother. The doctor was so relieved at the unexpected outcome that he came and took some fruits in the Ashram. The next day he came, together with his wife, and took initiation from Gurudev. Both became devoted disciples. Gurudev's love for cows is special, he says that a cow is the beauty of an Ashram. It is more difficult to materialize this wish in the United States or in Austria.

Cow, in Bengali and Oriya, is called "Goru". A spiritual master is called "Guru". Guru and Goru, the Master and the cow. Gurudev often teased us saying that Guru and Goru are one. Just as the external cow gives milk, Guru gives the milk of spiritual knowledge. Gurudev is like a prodigal cow, giving love to every disciple.

Role of the Guru

One day Gurudev called me, "Do you know what is the role of a Guru? A Guru gives *artha*, material success and *paramartha*, spiritual excellence, to his disciples. A Guru does not limit himself to giving a *mantra* or a technique or sharing his spiritual wealth. A Guru is one who will take care of his disciples' every need. A Guru is at the disciples' side when problems and difficulties arise."

I myself have seen Gurudev helping disciples in every step of life. He loves and serves them in an all-encompassing way. In the Guru Gita it is said, "There are many Gurus who look at the material achievements of the disciples so that they will derive some personal benefit. But there are a few rare Gurus who lift away the difficulties and problems that a disciple might face."

The Divine Gardener

Gurudev is a gifted gardener. He loves his garden, and gives careful attention to the flowers and fruits in all his different Ashrams, both in India and in the West. When he comes to each Ashram, he moves from one corner to the other, looking at the garden, taking note of how the plants have grown and guiding his disciples on how to make the garden even more beautiful.

Gurudev is not only a gardener in the outside world, he wants us to cultivate our inner garden too. The Garden of God should bloom with beautiful human beings that are filled with love, peace and purity. His admiration for God's creation is manifested in the garden. Gurudev is not only a gardener externally, he is a gardener spiritually. A parallel is created between the inner and outer spheres.

Years ago when we lived in the Karar Ashram, with its sandy soil, it was very important to water the plants every evening. There was no pipe connection, so we had to carry water in buckets from the hand pump. Gurudev would look on the whole procedure with a beatific smile, full of encouragement. It was really a beautiful experience.

Until now in Homestead, Florida, Gurudev takes care of the garden. He loves the fruits, trees and flowering plants. He has a whole team of devoted disciples that listen carefully to his instructions.

Once he told me that if a tree can give neither fruit nor flower, it is of less value. So also each spiritual person should try to give as much as he can to the rest of humanity.

Gurudev was fond of comparing a spiritual person with the fruit of a tree. If the fruit was small, it was useless. When it dropped from the tree, still unripe, it was lost and wasted. But if the fruit remained attached to the tree, slowly it would grow, ripen, and its color, smell and taste would evolve and change. When it was really ripe, it detached itself gently from the tree. People turn towards a tree full of ripe fruit. A Guru is like such a tree, and the disciple is the fruit. A tree is known by the fruit it bears.

His Love for the Holy Scriptures

Gurudev's mastery of World Scriptures as well as his interpretation of these holy texts is truly unique. On his bedside table lies a book of the Gita, a collection of the Upanishads and the Bible. Every day of his life he reads a few verses from these Holy Scriptures. He encouraged me to study the scriptures and to meditate upon them. Once he asked me if I had read the Bhagavad Gita by Lahiri Mahasaya. I had read a more contemporary version, but Baba had in his possession a very old edition of the book which had no beginning, no end, and the name of the author was not even mentioned. One evening after meditation, Gurudev surprised me with a very precious volume, written in Bengali. The book was so old, that the pages were almost crumbling. I was delighted with the book. It was really one of the most wonderful books on the Gita I had ever read. I read and translated the book simultaneously into Oriya, so as not to loose any of the benefits. Usually, I worked when everyone else was fast asleep. After several nights' work, I finished the book and filled with gratitude about having had such a treasure in my hands, I went to return it. Gurudev very graciously told me to keep it. But I declined, since I had made a translation, other people could have access to the text. Gurudev was happy, he even wanted me to print my notes.

When I came to Vienna in 1994, Baba told me to keep the valuable edition in my care. Not only is it an old and rare book, it also contains a few notes in Gurudev's handwriting. I treasure this rare gift.

His Joyful Mood

Once Gurudev had brought me to the West, I heard him talking about me to some disciples in a playful way, "Do you know what he is? He is an avocado. Not only does he like avocado, he is an avocado. An avocado is not so attractive in color, and sometimes an avocado is very small in size, but if you open it, it is so nutritious, full of food value and he is like that. Take care of him. You will get spiritual wealth from this small little avocado." All the Viennese disciples were enjoying this outburst of good humor, so he continued, "Don't let him go back to India. Keep the avocado with you, it can fit in your pocket, it is very small."

Much along the same line is another anecdote. During my monk's initiation, I had to shave my head, so for some time my hair was very short. When we had come back to Vienna, Gurudev told some disciples to bring some twigs, so that I would look like an ancient baba with tangled hair. Then much later, when my hair and beard grew long, he said jokingly, "Look, his beard and hair are really nice, but they are black. Should we dye them gray, then he would make much more of an impact." Everyone was smiling.

The Revered Teacher

Gurudev is a careful listener. When he hears something new and noteworthy, he scribbles all valuable information in a small notebook. This illustrates Gurudev's permanent desire to learn new things, without any personal ego. He also graciously gives credit to the source, when he uses it at a later stage. Baba often quoted a Bengali proverb that says, 'If you see some ashes somewhere, look beneath the ash and find the treasure.' He kept insisting that the real meaning was, 'Do not neglect anyone's ideas, underneath could lie some great spiritual truth.'

Gurudev is a unique spiritual Master, who teaches in every step of life. He wants to bring transformation to the life of each disciple. He always gave me clear-cut guidelines; asking me to always keep them in mind. In order to lead a spiritual life it was crucial to follow these instructions:

- Practice for perfection.
- Never waste time.
- Never be entangled in politics.
- Keep the mind always anchored in the divine.
- Be loyal to the Guru.
- Have love for the Guru.
- Give love to all, irrespective of the situation at hand.

I am permanently trying to follow his guidance. Gurudev has handed down a wealth of spiritual knowledge. My gratitude and devotion knows no bounds.

A Momentous Occasion

For many years no one outside my immediate family knew my date of birth. Although many people asked, I avoided giving an answer. The date of birth in my passport comes from school records and it is not correct. When some disciples, glancing at my passport would seek confirmation, I would smile and say, "No, that is not my birthday, it is just the date of birth in my passport."

I was therefore very surprised when on the 10th of August, 1996, while I was in a program with Gurudev in Zurich, everyone, following

Baba's cue sang 'Happy Birthday'. Until then I was unaware that Gurudev knew my date of birth.

One year later, I was in Portland, Oregon. I spent most of the day meditating and I got only a few phone calls from some disciples in Europe.

In 1998, on the 10th of August, I was in Cleveland, Ohio for a program in the house of a disciple, Dr. Harinath Bathina and his family. That day in the morning they had a special ceremony for my birthday, and during that time the telephone rang. We all were in prayer and meditation and did not answer the telephone. But I could hear the voice of Gurudev, he was sending me a birthday message, "Today is a most auspicious day, it is the birthday of Paramahamsa Prajnanananda. Today I confer all my blessings as Paramahamsa."

After meditation and prayer we listened to the recorded message. It was really a surprise. I could not understand if Gurudev had mentioned Paramahamsa Prajnanananda by mistake. After some time, the telephone rang again and it was from Vienna. When I picked up the receiver, Gurudev was telling me, "From today I give you the title of 'Paramahamsa'. So you are no more Swami Prajnanananda, from today you are Paramahamsa Prajnanananda."

I was unable to talk. I had tears in my eyes as I thought, "Until now you are a mystery to me. I have not understood who you are." The image of Yoganandaji flashed through my mind. What had I done to be worthy of such a great honor? Slowly I recovered my voice and was able to murmur, "I am not worthy of all these things. I bow to you, my Guru! Let me seek your love, your blessing. I am overwhelmed. Let this life be used for a divine purpose and let this life be like a flower, offered at the feet of the Guru, the sacred feet of God. Let every breath, every thought, every word be used for fulfilling this mission. Let my life be filled with self-sacrifice, self-oblation, let my life be the oil that is offered as an oblation. I bow to God, I bow to my Guru. Let me be your tool."

My life, I realized, had become inextricably bound with that of my beloved Master and his lineage. As my spiritual father, Gurudev had opened the door to a future weighed down with responsibilities. I only hope I will prove to be a worthy pupil of such a rare, loving and unique Master. We have been welded in a relationship that has no beginning and no end.

Who Are You?

Gurudev is always absorbed in divine love. Perhaps one of the most moving moments I have experienced in his presence was when he has initiated some of his disciples into monk-hood.

While washing their feet, I have witnessed the outflow of pure love emanating from Gurudev. Baba's love is unique. Throughout my life I have seen the endless amount of love he pours on his disciples. I have never met anyone who is so loving, so caring, so attentive to every detail.

The relationship with one's Guru transcends all time and place, it is eternal. In many countless instances in my life, when he has been physically far away, I have felt his helping hand at a moment of need, when a kind stranger has suddenly appeared to assist me. Some would think it a coincidence, I have known it to be the silent, benevolent, living presence of my Guru.

There are many unusual episodes I could recount. His letters have reached me without a proper address. While I was in Germany, I received a letter addressed to Triloki Brahmachari c/o the name of my host in Hamburg, Germany. Then again when I was teaching in India, I also got a letter from Baba who was in America at that time, with the following address,

Triloki Das, Ravenshaw College, India.

Ravenshaw College has nearly 7.000 students and about 300 faculty members, there was no mention of which Department I worked in, no street address, no mention of the city or the post code. Still the letter reached my hands. Many amazing things happen with a realized Master.

Baba is always concerned for his disciples but he never interferes in their destiny. Once there was a lady who requested Gurudev to intercede on her behalf with her father-in-law. When he declined, she became somewhat insistent until Gurudev told her many past events that were behind her present difficulties. The lady in question became a very sincere and devoted follower, through meditation she was able to find her own answers and improve her condition.

A long time ago, back in the days of the Puri Ashram, an elderly mother disciple slipped a little piece of paper underneath Gurudev's pillow, just before he retired. On it she had written only one question in Bengali, '*Baba, Tumi Ke*', which means 'Baba, Who are you?' Sometime, during his sleep, Baba had written '*Ami Bhagavan*' or 'I am God'.

Guru is a manifestation of God. "Gu" means the invisible One or God, "Ru" means what is visible. The invisible God uses what is visible as his instrument. A true Master is responsible for his disciples until they reach liberation. He will guide them in all spheres of life, remove their bad *karma* and lowest propensities, and lead them towards the path of light.

When a disciple is pure and sincere in his search for liberation, God will send him an illumined Master.

The principles of the Holy Scriptures are manifested more in a realized Master. Through the guidance of the Guru we can rise above body-consciousness and perceive the living presence of God within us and in all our surroundings.

Baba Hariharanandaji is the embodiment of spiritual truth, love and compassion. Not even the holiest scripture can substitute the encompassing influence of an enlightened Master.

I bow to God again and again with the utmost gratitude for allowing me to have the good fortune to serve such a Master.

Psalm of Life

Lives of great men all remind us
We can make our life sublime,
And departing leaves behind us
Footprints on the sands of time.

Footprints that perhaps another
Sailing over life's solemn main
A forlorn and shipwrecked brother
Seeing, shall take heart again.

Let us then be up and doing
With a heart for any fate
Still achieving, still pursuing
Learn to labor and to wait.

H.W. Longfellow

13. Arrival in Vienna, 27th of April, 1995

14. Final instructions before departing to India

15. First visit to the USA, 1996

16. In New York

17. Serving Baba

18. Birthday celebration, 1996

19. Bidding farewell, Tattendorf 1998

20. Sharing a special moment

21. Divine oneness in the ocean of cosmic consciousness.

22. Together in India, March 1996

23. The father and the son, walking together

SECTION II

- Reflections of My Master's Mind -

Compilation of Selected Letters from Gurudev to Triloki Dash

Epilogue

Pure love is unconditional and flows directly from the heart to encompass all aspects of our life. When we come in touch with this kind of love, our life is transformed, we constantly experience inexpressible joy.

Such is the bond between the Guru and the disciple. When I came in contact with my Master, my life began to be transformed. I had a constant yearning to be in his presence, to serve him, to learn from him. I felt such peace and bliss sitting and meditating near him, that my soul would constantly roam in God-consciousness.

It was impossible to be always in the physical company of Gurudev. He was a traveling monk, a *vishvaguru,* a world teacher. His mission was to care for many seeking souls. I often felt the pain of separation until I fully realized our oneness.

When I first started corresponding with Gurudev, it was without any expectation. A subtle spiritual rejuvenation would fill me as I wrote. Since no sincere endeavor remains unfulfilled, he wrote me back, and my heart would leap in joy at the sight of his small, beautifully formed hand-writing.

For a decade we exchanged hundreds of letters. His were full of inspiration, teachings, understanding and encouragement. Mine were full of submission and surrender.

I have treasured each small piece of paper, sometimes containing only a few lines. It is difficult for me to describe the enormous impact that Gurudev had in my life.

A few selected letters have been presented here. Some have been slightly modified, deleting the more personal references. Others have been printed in their original form. All of them portray the boundless love that unites us.

If we can occupy a position in the vast and all-encompassing heart of a divine Master, through a selfless and dedicated life, a disciplined and devoted behavior, a generous spiritual outlook; our life will reflect his image and we will at last become worthy disciples.

From,
H. Giri

AUM

I hope you all are well. I am improving.

The money which you have sent for honest cause, God has seen your mind and he is happy for it and will give more money to you.

Every human being is the power of God. God is hiding in every human head in the cerebral-cortex, *sahasra dala padma* in atom point, see Svetasvetara Upanisad VI.11. God is all-pervading. He is the indwelling self of every human being, and He is inhaling through the nostrils of every human being, and He is doing all types of work (1) money, (2) sex, (3) food, (4) in the heart good and bad, (5) in the neck center many types of religions - many sects, cult creed but all are extrovert. But Kriya Yoga is not extrovert. It is introvert. Only by technique *yoga karmasu kaushalam*.[1] Just the Aeroplane is climbing up from the ground with technique.

God is inhaling from our birthday. We all are the power of God. He is our life. He is constantly inhaling, even when you are sleeping. He is formless, even in the body that formless body is activating.

In short I am telling about Kriya Yoga.

1st you will feel your own pulse and then you bow, watch, which is throbbing in the pulse, that something is moving in your *sahasrara*. In the middle where the softness of the baby's head you fix your attention there. Then you must feel that pulsation. Calmly watch.

Keep your tongue rolled up, with a very short breath, search that *sahasrara* (2). Then you will feel God movement sensation and divine sound there.

Keep keenest attention in *sahasrara* then you will feel snow white light all over the universe, in this stage you can get *samadhi*.

Also love Him. The almighty father is hiding in the cerebral-cortex.

Only deepest love is required! Because He is inhaling from your birthday.

So God-realisation is your birthright.

For God-realisation you do not require any flowers, fruits or sweets. Your heart is your only flower. If you can give your heart then you will get no sense of the body and you are giving everything.

If you only keep your attention and feel that God movement sensation on the top, then you will feel God movement sensation in your whole body, divine sound in the whole body and divine light in the whole world and give divine love to formless father, who is hiding in your whole body and in the whole world.

Love, Love, Love, Love.

In your practical life watch the power of God is activating, watch Him whole day and night.

I want to bow you all

Humble, H. Giri

Do not tear my letter. Read several times in your whole life. One day you will feel the value of the letter. If possible come to me for two days and you will learn more.

---

1 Yoga is skill in action. For detail, see the Gita II.50.

To,
Triloki Dash, Karar Ashram
Swargadwar, Puri, Orissa.

My inseparable Soul!

What is the news? Your mind is constantly engrossed in Soul. Whether you are watching that you are constantly merged in Him? Whether you are feeling that you are not separated from Almighty Father. Whether you are watching in going breath and out coming breath which is pulled by Him? If you constantly feel it then you can get constant *jagrad samadhi*.[1] Through this one gets constant liberation and constant alertness. If there is light there is no darkness. My eyes are operated. After operation I am able to see clearly. *atma jagarane vayam nasti.* Who will bless whom? The One who is within you, will bless you. Practice Kriya nicely, O my dear child. You have come to this world and you are to leave it. Have you thought over it?

Humble Hariharananda

---

1 *jagrad samadhi* is a state of inner awakening, when one experiences a blissful state of divine communion, while in wakeful state of activity.

2 A Sanskrit proverb describing, that eternal vigilance is the price of liberty.

To,
Triloki Dash,
Karar Ashram, Swargadwar,
Puri,Orissa.

My One Soul, My affectionate and divine Soul.

It is my desire that all my divine power and spiritual knowledge and my divine brain will enter in your whole system. No one is near me, who can receive my vast divine knowledge and can merge in truth means *samadhi* stage. Desire of every person to reach the divine goal, you have also the same, but your desire and destiny is too great. Meditate and watch God in every moment of your life.

Blessings for all

Humble Hariharananda

From,
H. Giri

To,
Triloki Dash, Lecturer in Economics,
Ravenshaw College,
Cuttack-3, Orissa.

My affectionate and divine Soul.

I am extremely happy to know, that you are always watching the power of God within you. As there is fire in the wood, so soul is hiding in the whole body wood. Seek Him, see Svetasvetara Upanisad I/15 and try your utmost and watch Him within. Inform your friend and tell him to meditate with you. You must earn spiritual wealth and divine wealth at a time.

Blessings for all. H. Giri

From,
H. Giri

To,
Triloki Dash,
Lecturer, Ravenshaw College,
Cuttack-3, Orissa.

My Divine Soul!

Your letter gave me your living presence. Your letter washed my body with divine joy.

Baba! God is all-pervading, so He is in every human body, even He is doing *kri + ya*, whole day in your body. If you watch breath and work, you are always realised and divine. Practice it constantly then you will get constant liberation. Every day I pray for you. From 22nd to 30th May c/o. Mark Sclafani ...

Blessings for all.

Humble H. Giri

From,
Swami Hariharananda Giri,
c/o. Mr. Felix Marquez,
300 E. 33rd Street
New York, NY 10016.

15.10.90

My affectionate and divine Triloki Baba!

... I am happy in any circumstance, I will only say Shriyukteshwarji, "Gurudev, thy will be done Guru, thy will be done."

I am old, I always keep my mind on God and Gurus. God and Gurus are very kind to me. They give me everything. What more I can expect. Every day I tell God - Lord still today you have kept me on the earth.

I do not feel my physical body, as if it is dead, only spiritual body is alive. Until you feel it sincerely, you cannot get God-realization. You should every moment watch that you are just an onion. Every day you open one skin from above. All the time you watch him, before and after and while performing an action. Constantly you watch - there is one invisible counter part in your each body part. Constantly you watch your all negative and in each negative you will seek God and avoid negative and avoid temptation.

Know thy self, presume not God to scan
Proper study of mankind is man

Alexander Pope.

Always watch Him, seek Him, touch Him, remain one with Him. Every moment He is changing you. Every two minutes time millions cells are dying. Practice 1st technique more and be free, be power of God. Real Guru is living mother "*ishwara gururatmeti...*"[1] Love. Love. Love your Guru, who is your living Durga.

I received your many letters which gave extreme joy, ... Answer is this. You are writing me so I am giving spiritual answer of your letter. If you read my letter your whole system will be covered with divinity. You can meditate more according to my spiritual guidance through letter.

Inform my affection, regard and blessings all you and your family, take my affection. Blessings for all.

Blessings, H. Giri

---

1 A stanza from the Dakshinamurti Stotra, explaining the unity of God, Guru and the Soul.

c/o Mr. Jerry Peabody, Ph.D.
... , CLOISTER Dr.
Rockville, MD. 20852, USA

To,
Triloki Das, Lecturer
Nuasahi, Jobra, Cuttack-753003, India.

22.11.90 New York

My affectionate and divine and One Soul Triloki Baba!

I hope you all are well. I am writing in lying posture. If I sit for 25 minutes, I get pain in my thigh joint and on right back.

I am happy because I am writing you. ...

... Now I feel better meditation. I hope I wrote you before.

The atom power of God/living power of God is pulling breath from within (the home of God), so you should sit there 3 inches inside, and when God will pull breath, then you realize that, you are getting touch of God. Love Him "*para bhakti diantu anande bibhora huantu*"[1] proceed forward and be like Lahiri Baba, get materialisation stage.

Always feel the power of God is within you, in every human being, and everywhere in the universe.

He created everything only for your joy and for your liberation.

Just you feel the stage of Chaitanya Mahaprabhu. If you always feel that you are detached and attached, whole day and night then, the power of God is activating not you.

... So I say "*sadhu sabadhana*" (Oh Monk, be careful) first *brahmacharya* ... ... you first finish your *brahmacharya* "*sarva kalvidam brahma*"[2]

... Proceed forward and to perceive the power of God is only remaining in you and constantly activating in you. Night and day night and day you are in me night and day.

... Here there is extreme cold outside, inside spring of India. Only one thin Ganji is enough, floor is covered with thick woollen carpet. Always hot water and there is no cold in the bathroom! I cannot go out.

I am well. I am revising and adding more in the *Bhagavadgita*. Today

I completed 5/13. A very important verse, like the stages of *muni-rishi.*

"*mama maya duratyaya*" but "*mameva ye prapadyante*"

Meditate, earn money, serve your parents, this is worship

"*chatur je mina sei to jane ma - jal theke je mukti achhe - tai jele jakham jal phele se - lukay jeler payer kachhe - jal ediye tai se banche ma.*"[4]

If you remain 3 inches deepest in the home of God then all negative may not go to the abode of God. That place is free "*yasnin gata na nivartante bhuyah*".

Meditate, meditate and meditate and always remain in the Atom point. In the abode of God. ...

... You must feel you are the living power of God, any letter you are reading, that is read by the power of God.

Everything in this world is the power of God. ...

Mary Magdalene is the best lady disciple of Jesus.

... Remain in the abode of God. You are a free bird in the free air. I bow everybody.

Humble.

Hariharananda

---

1 Written in Oriya, meaning, give Supreme love to God and be in blissful state.

2 This is a great saying of the Upanishads, explaining that everything is nothing but the manifestation of the Divine.

3 See the Gita VII.14.

4 A Bengali song on the Divine Mother. The intelligent fish knows how to be free from the net of the fisher man. If it comes closer to his feet then he is free.

From,
Swami Hariharanda Giri
c/o. Mr. Felix Marquez,
... 33rd Street
New York, NY 10016

To,
Triloki Das
Nua- Sahi. Jobra,
Cuttack - 3, Orissa,
India.

7.12.90

My divine Triloki Baba!

Without thc power of God, this pen cannot move. So you should read my letter and watch that your real you is seeing me and your real you is reading letter.

Best meditation is to watch Him through your work, watch that you are the real power of God and the living Power of God.

Until you watch *ham* + *sa* then in your practical life you will get divine change what is the difference between you and the other people of the world. Always watch you are special power of God. Sending one Soul Culture life of Jesus.

What is speciality in you? You are feeling you are living power of God means you are in the door of God *sarva dvāreṣu kaunteya* ... ... XIV.11, V.13, VIII.12 in the Gita. You are two at a time. So you can never make any mistake. Because when you are always remaining in the open door of God, how negative can come. The moment you will see negative you watch Gita IV.42. *jāgarane bhayam nāsti*.

... I do not like the word heaven because I am far beyond of it. I am always inside the door of liberation *kṣine punye martya lokam viśanti*.[1]

Meditate and keep Hariharananda in your whole system.

What more you want. One ounce of practice is worth tons of theories.

Watch night and day, night and day you are alert in me night and day.

I am well. God has brought his baby child H. Giri and keeping him on His lap.

You all take my deepest affection and blessings of God and Gurus.

Humble Hariharananda

...

1 See the Gita IX.21, that describes the fruits of *karma* (action).

My affectionate and divine Triloki Baba!

Pranam to you and to all
esho nava nava rupe esho prane
gandhe rase rupe shabde gane[1]
mane hoche ami bhalo achhi, mane hoche abar ami javo, avar gaan sekhabro, ar sabai drita bhagavan pathe agiye nebo.[2]

You all watch God constantly. I am always with you. See that I am meditating through your body. See B. Gita XIII.14.15.16 ... ...

Blessings for all.

Humble Hariharananda

---

1 This is a letter written after Durga Puja, in the month of October. It is a song in which Mother Durga is invoked, to manifest Herself in one's life and all senses.

2 This part is written in Bengali. The meaning is, 'I think I am better, I think I will go again. I will teach you to sing and will guide everyone to progress quickly in the path of God-realisation.'

From,
H. Giri

21.1.91

I am extremely happy to receive your letter. Almost every day I think of you due to 7 lights inside the spine. That is *sapta loka* (seven planes of existence), 7 fires, 7 oblations, 5 types of thought.[1]

Now I almost do not talk and stay on the 6th fire and try to become free from worldly senses. But world is so crafty, vicious, corrupt, you can not tackle with them.

Jesus, Socrates and Mahatma Gandhi were so sacrificing but they all got extreme trouble, even death. But as Jesus did not die because he was son of God so he came back from death. This humble insignificant Hariharananda can not be compared with them, but he gave and is giving real guidance to his advancement and also giving extreme affection, regard and oneness to all persons.

I will reach Cuttack on 6th March morning and will remain in the house of Chaturbhuj Rangalal (Modi). Tell them to come to receive me in Cuttack station. I will write in what train I will go and what time I will reach. Tell everybody also. Tell Chaturbhuj Baba on 17th March, I will go to Puri and he will take me with his car. If he cannot, tell Niranjan Baba to arrange.

Breath is the living power of God so with faint breath watch Him always, watch your body is your living power of God. Be very careful about negative. If there is light there will be no darkness.

I am improving but pain is still there. You all are my living God, so I bow every body.

Humble Hariharananda

---

1 See Mundaka Upanishad II.1.8

From,
H. Giri

26th Feb. 91

My affectionate and divine Triloki Baba!

I received your three divine letters which is heart touching, sweet and divine.

You are the only real seeker of God and you have studied Upanishad, Patanjali, Bhagavad Gita, Brahma Sutra even many authentic spiritual books and no one except you. So in your life you must get *nirvikalpa samadhi*. Only it depends on greatest desire. Your whole life will be peaceful and wealthy.

Any word or letter I am writing, I am watching the power of God is writing through my hand and I am feeling divine joy. So you read my letter and watch that living power of God is reading letter through your soul. This is soul culture.

... You can get constant alertness. Then, your spiritual foundation will be very strong. In every letter I am writing I am getting divineness. Who is writing? Dead body? Or two bodies. So when divine body is the soul doer then why should we forget Him. Try. Try. Try constantly.

You are pure, sweet, kind, loving, generous, broad-minded. This is the sign of a Guru. See Gita 2nd chapter 50th verse, then up to the end.

Baba! I wrote one letter on 8th Feb. I did not post it because I thought I will go to India in the beginning of March, it is why I did not post it. Now I am sure I will not go due to my eye operation.

... I humbly request you please give it to all newspapers that eye of Swami Hariharananda Giri will be operated in April so in this year he will not be in Puri Annual function on 22nd March, 91.

So you must give it to the newspapers. Please think deeply and do it.

You please go to the house of Goldsmith Baba to guide him.

You will always get my guidance from the distance. Hariharananda is always sitting in the whole body of Triloki Baba.

You all take my deepest affection and enjoy blessing of God and Gurus.

Humble Hariharananda

PS, Please hear English news of Calcutta or Delhi and correct your pronunciation. Keep it in a notebook and correct.

From,
Swami H. Giri,
Lyzanne Peabody,
... Cloister Dr., Rockville, MD 20852,
To,
Triloki Dash, Lecturer,
Nua sahi Jobra, Cuttack-3, Orissa, India.

Triloki

I am extremely happy to receive many heart touching letters from you.

2) This is the first time I came to know from you what Lingaraj Baba said about the case.

3) Sure I felt, wherever you spoke, your speech was top heart touching speech. Surely God will make you top great speaker in Kriya Yoga line, even any subject you will speak.

4) Your spiritual study and meditation will make you real realized person.

5) Always burn the ego. Always read and remember Gita 4th chapter 37-42 verses. This will be your life and whole 5th chapter "*karma sannyasa*" also will be your life.[1]

What is the top spirituality in the world? If you constantly watch the power of God is always pulling breath through your nose, so you are God in human being. You are the living power of God. Even you constantly watch, when you are forgetting that you are the living power of God. Always apply the Gita 5th chapter 8th and 9th verses in your every action.

7)You are true seeker, so you studied me through and through. I try to keep me in divine stage so ... ... You know fully that I have no attachment in money. If I can spend money on honest work, I think myself fortunate. So I am quite free of the negative. You are also the same. You gave me Joy-time piece[2]. Every day I see you through the Joy-time piece. Also you are generous according to your limit. I am the unlimited company not ego but it is a teaching for you all.

My real wealth is my alertness in the inner self. So you please take share of my spiritual wealth. As much as you can.

I am a free bird in the free air. What ever I take eat I say I am giving oblation to the third fire *vaishvanara agni* [3]. Be very careful of 2nd fire and 4th fire, *ahavaniya agni* [4]. You read the letter of Satyandra Baba[5] make it photocopy and put it in "*patravali*" also you make photocopy of your letter and send it to ... ... give it to the magazine.

What is the result of all religions ? Answer is PEACE.

What is the main achievement in your life ? To know thyself. If you know thyself then your all negatives will disappear. This is the main gain in your life "*mayam tu prakriti viddhim mayinam tu maheshwara.*"[6] Be careful of *maya, moha, bhranti.*[7] My eye will be operated work will start from 7th April 91 investigation up to 15th every examination then 15th eye operation.

So on 7th March 91 please give to all newspapers that Swami Hariharananda Giri's eye will be operated in America New York so Swamiji will not remain in Annual Function 22nd March 91. ...

Heart felt blessings for all.

I want to bow all persons, this is my pleasure.

Humble Hariharananda

---

1 O Arjuna! (Bharata) With the sword of knowledge cut out all the ignorance that remains in your heart. Be free from doubt and practice the yoga of action and yoga of knowledge. Don't be heart broken. Stand up and fight with your ignorance (Gita IV.42). The entire fifth chapter of the Gita speaks of the life of a renunciate person.

2 Joy-time piece is a gift of an alarm-clock presented to Gurudev by Triloki.

3 The fire in the navel center.

4 The fire in the heart center.

5 The pre-monastic name of Swami Brahmananda.

6 A *mantra* from the Shvetashvetara Upanishad (IV.10), meaning, know then that *prakriti* is *maya* and the wielder of *maya* is the Great Lord.

7 Delusion, *maya*, illusion and error.

From,
S.H.G.
Lyzanne Peabody,
... Cloister Dr.
Rockville, M D 20852

AUM

BALABHADRA-M A- JAGANNATH

U

SUBHADRA

28th of March

Crucifixion day of Jesus.

My affectionate and divine Triloki Baba!

I am extremely happy to receive Bhagavad Gita and Tribhashi from you. I am astonished that this Gita is available in Cuttack.

I hope, the annual function of Shriyukteswar's Karar Ashram was finished successfully. I am happy to know that you gave it in three newspapers.

Even it is given in the invitation letter, that Gurudev will not come due to his eye operation.

Now I request you if you once come to America then just now you make your passport in Bhubaneshwar Passport Office. In this affairs the sister's husband Radhanath Rath, he was the authority.

Lingaraj Rath Baba and Dr. Radhanath Rath Baba they are very close friends. So you please talk with Lingaraj Rath Baba, by which he will request Radhanath Rath who will help you to get your passport quickly.

So, if you have the wish to come in the foreign country, then proceed quickly. Then you can come in USA during the summer vacation or Puja vacation.

I also repeatedly told you to hear the English news from Delhi and Calcutta Center, then you can get accurate pronunciation.

Lyzanne Ma said, I talked with Triloki Baba, his pronunciation is almost good.

"desha bhramana hela prakruta shiksha."[1] ... ...

Meditate and watch your every breath. As inside the egg; the eyes, bill, fur, legs and nail of the bird are remaining, so in the egg of God,[2] three inches inside, you get moment sensation of the soul. You only remain in the soul and from that atom point watch breath is in the soul, and also teeth, mouth, chin, neck, heart, stomach, everything is moving from above from the atom point. In this way you teach the students.

I am daily reducing. My body weight from 152 lbs. at present to 140 lbs. Body resistance is gone. I am writing this much letter, my blood pressure has come down to 140/85 to 110/78.

"je kare amar ash ami kari sarvanash."[3]

Blessings of God and Gurus and my humble love affection and regard.

Humble Hariharananda

This is my handwriting and signature.

---

1 This is written in Oriya, the language spoken in the State of Orissa, meaning, knowledge expands by travelling in different countries

2 Egg of God, in Sanskrit Brahmanda, symbolizing the entire creation.

3 It is a Bengali proverb, saying that God tries the devotees in many ways.

17th July 91

My One Soul, Triloki Baba!

I read your 4 letters, but at that time I was extremely unwell. So I wrote you only with my minds pen.

Most important I am sending one cassette you please hear it in presence of all. ...

Meditate means be God.

"*Deha - dehi - evam videha - purushottam*."[1] Try to feel you are living God. Only remain in the atom, merged, be one, love and realize. You are always living power of God.

I say some times during time of food you feel you are doing *puja* of your *ishta*. You are *ishta. ishta* in atom point love, love, love *prema-paranurakti* [2]

Get ready to come in foreign country. I am sending one lecture ... ... and please see the pronunciation. This is the beauty in speech. Although many things he left and in the beginning unnecessarily he explains *brahmanandam*.

Pranams, Blessings

Humble H. Giri

---

1 *deha* means body, *dehi* means the Soul and *videha purushottama* means the Supreme Lord, the Creator in a formless state. This three constitute our life.

2 This is a quotation from the Bhakti Sutra of Shandilya (the Aphorisms on Divine Love, written by the sage Shandilya), which explains divine love is experiencing oneness with *Ishwara*, God.

From,
Swami H. Giri
c/o Mr. Don Abram,
... Riverside Drive 85th,
NY- 10028 USA.

To,
Triloki Das
Nua Sahi, Jobra,
CUTTACK – 3.

1st August 91

My divine father Triloki Baba!

I hope you all are well. I am okay. Today I want to know what is the name of first son of Matsyagandha by whom Drtarastra and Pandu were born. You are the only person who can write me about it.

My memory is down 5 days. I am trying to remember it, but it is not possible to remember.

Short cut way to God-realisation is to bow and to search inside the atom-point. Breath will be very feeble, even not *nasabhyāntara cārinau*. Gita V.27.

Only search and research. Be free from everything, this is God-realisation. Whether you are realised, *avang manasa gocara* stage. In the practical life always two, body and Soul as if I am not I, I am that real I. Body + Soul are one.

Whole day and night you are the real You and always remain free from temptation. If you want to kill yourself, a little poison is enough, but to kill other person you require many things. So try to kill your own ego and watch you are realised. My pranams to you and to all. Inform my Oneness with every person. Many times a day I think of you because you are after truth. ...

... So I am not thinking of you now. Maybe my eye will be operated in the end of August. Pranams to everybody, if God takes me to his holy unknown lap, I will be happy. All well that ends well ...

My life, is a complete life.

Please post the letter to Dharanidhar Pakhara Baba and hand over other two letters to the proper persons.

Triloki Baba - you are my only advanced, real disciple, who has through study on Gita, Upanishad Patanjali some Brahma Sutra etc. some study. You are the true seeker of God. You are a Brahmin and you know about Puja. *Havana paddhati*[1] also you have extreme idea of spiritual realised persons of Orissa, and you studied their books.

You are the only person who wants to get God-realisation. Also you both even Joynarayan and Raghabananda have love, extreme love on Guru and God, you want soul culture. You are the only person who is vastly learned in scriptures so I love you very deeply and I cherish regard on you, because you are really true seeker of God. I always pray for you all.

Real true seeker, when he will meditate, he will follow Gita V.27, even you are not watching breath during the time of meditation. As if you are dead *yoga nidra*.

Even breathlessness stage *apare niyata ahara*, means in this way you will get *nirvikalpa samadhi*.

But during the time of work, you always watch you and the power of God are working together. You are not giving lecture in the college or you are not conducting meditation class you and your life both together are doing it. In seven centres you watch Him you and life of God are doing work together. Breath (oxygen) maintains life fire. Isha Upanishad 17-18 are at our life, it is air *vayuh ... ... anilam* are *amritam*.

Through feeble breath *bhasmantam shariram*, so constantly think *krato* and constantly remain alert *krtam* means any work you are doing it is done by Him. Night and day He is for you. Then 18 verse. The fire is our life, that fire is maintained by the breath *vayu* 17th verse.

During Diwali, 14 lights are inside the spine, 14 fires, 7 ascending, 7 descending, good and bad. Ascending is good, opposite is bad. So always say *naya ma supatha*, O God my life, please lead me by the divine road. O God, you know all my bad qualities. Please save me like Ratnakara and Vilvamangala. My forgetfulness is my sin. Please save me from it and give me constant alertness and *nitya mukta avastha*.

Whole day and night you watch your indwelling self, like Hariharananda, and remain free from vanity, then you can quickly and constantly get God hood.

Please make a photocopy and send it to ... ... they should give it to the magazine.

I am so happy here. I am free from everything. I am constantly absorbed in Soul.

My eye will be operated in August, and then in Sept., I will go to India and mostly stay with you, or you will stay with me.

I humbly request you that all the fruits of H. Giri tree, will be like Hariharananda.

I bow all

Humble H. Giri

---

1 The ceremonial procedure for a fire ceremony, strictly observed by the qualified priests.

Triloki Dash,
Karar Ashram, Swargadwar Rd.
Puri, Orissa.

My affectionate and divine Triloki Baba!

Almost every day I think of you and I pray for you because you were reading my letters and taking quickest dictation and writing many letters. No one can take so quickest dictation. Please meditate deeply. Whole day in practical life watch that God is doing work. But during the time of meditation, you should remain in formless stage. Go beyond light, sound and vibration. Because soundless stage will lead you to the truth. Only intangible nothingness. As if you are sleeping but not sleep "*na tatra caksu gacchati*."[1]

12th Aug. right eye operation.

You all take my blessings, affection. ... ... will stay here

Humble Hariharananda

---

1 See Kena Upanishad I.3, There the eye goes not, speech goes not, nor the mind; we know not, we understand not how one can teach this.

Triloki Dash,

Karar Ashram, Swargadwar Rd.
Puri, Orissa.

Gomamse anurag. If you get *khechari* then *mukti* (liberation). *Bharya niye sarva tyaga*. If you feel detached then *mukti* (liberation). *Guru marle swarga vas*. If you can be free from two bodies, then *mukti* (liberation). *Hari bhajale sarvanasha*. If you go and reach formless stage, then *mukti* (liberation)[1]. *Vijaya* greetings.

Be detached. Be free from two bodies. Reach the formless stage. I am well. This letter is for all. Doctor says no read no write but eye is ok.

H. Giri

---

1 This is a popular yogic proverb in Bengali with a dual meaning. The ordinary meaning is, 'Love to take beef. Be attached to your wife. Keep Guru in trouble and if you pray to God than all difficulties will come.' But the inner meaning is explained by Gurudev.

From,
H. Giri

To,
Triloki Das
Nua Sahi, Jobra,
Cuttack - 3, Orissa.

My affectionate and divine Triloki Baba!

Causal - A, Astral - U, Gross - M = Om Baba! or Jagannath, Shubhadra and Balaram,

3 bodies Baba!

Only your deepest desire for meditation and liberation and whole day. Gita VIII. 14 *ananya ceta sarvatrah*, whole day and night always and constantly who watches me through natural breath and practical work - He is activating in you. If they with love remain alert in me, I am easily obtainable to them. So complete your course and get God-realisation and liberation.

Realisation 1st then Ashram. I am happy to know that Government is willing to give land for Ashram. ...

... I am gaining body weight but back pain is more. Please write me in detail specially your work in Ravenshaw College.

You all take the blessings of God and Gurus

Humble H. Giri

From,
Swami Hariharananda Giri,
c/o. Virginia Barry,
... W 47 St.,
New York City, USA.

17th June 92

My affectionate and divine Triloki Baba!

I am extremely happy to receive your two letters. I am writing many letters to you through my mind's pen.

Specially I want to know what is about your transfer.

I pray to God by which you can stay in Cuttack, and can go in many places to spread Kriya Yoga. Kriya Yoga is a scientific technique like a fax machine, Kriya Yoga can remove body sense and world sense in one minute time. In the open meeting I say and I call one person and within one minute I am giving movement sensation of the power of God in one minute, and divine sensation, divine sound and divine light.

Just below the occipital bone there are two very small holes from that place 12 cranial nerves are flowing in five sense organs and in the whole body which give extreme extrovert stages to all human beings, that is *kundalini*.

pindam kundalini shakti which means our gross body is full of *maya* delusion. So all human beings are restless and in extrovert stage.

Only if all human beings bow 7 times then that influence of 12 cranial nerves will come up to the soul and all human beings in 2 minutes time will get calmness, which is Godliness.

Kriya Yoga is a scientific technique. In a few minutes they will be able to hear divine sound, *ishta mantra* also will feel the life movement sensation of *ishta mantra* in the 50 body parts which is called *matrika nyasa*, also ignorance of human beings will be transformed in super conscious stage and cosmic conscious stage. They might be able to attain wisdom.

prajnam brahma

Wisdom cannot be realised by the 5 sense organs.

naiva vaca na manasha [1]

No one has control over the 12 cranial nerves, only a realised Yogi, who gets *samadhi* stage, that is wisdom.

So practice Kriya Yoga very deeply and constantly watch Him in your practical work, then you will get constant liberation. See the Bhagavad Gita 6th chapter 31st verse

sarvatha vartamanopi sa yogi mayi vartate.[2]

I am happy to know that there will be a Kriya Yoga Center in Cuttack.

...

Write me ...

I will remain there from 15th July to 25th July.

I am physically better, gained body weight but pain is still remaining.

Inform my love, pranams to everybody. Special *pranams* to your parents.

athava yoginameva kule bavathi dimata.[3]

Gita VI.41,42

Thank you I want to bow you all ... again I say, *nama namastetu sahasrarkrtvah.*[4]

Humble Hariharananda

---

1 Please see, Katha Upanishad II.3.12 meaning; 'not by speech, not by mind, not by sight can the Soul be experienced.'

2 Devotees with a balance of mind, who watch Me everywhere, who perceive Me in everything, and who don't judge anything, are the real Yogis. In the world, in all circumstances, they always abide in Me.

3 Or they might be born into the family of a learned Yogi, but that birth is undoubtedly very rare in this world.

4 See the Gita XI.39, Salutations to You a thousand times.

3rd of Dec. 92

My affectionate and divine Triloki Baba!

Just now I am receiving your letter ... ...

My back-pain is my lifelong friend. There is a little crack in the disc in between money center and sex center on the 4th vertebra and 5th vertebra.

One mother she was also getting this pain. Her son is an Engineer. That mother gave me a waist-belt that is helping to me. They made it in Cuttack. Do you know the shop? If not ask them and tell the shopkeeper to make only two steel plates for me not the full belt.

I have one nice belt made in Germany. I will give it to the shopkeeper and he will fix it there.

I will remain very short period in Cuttack only 18th and 19th on 20th March I will go to Puri.

Meditate deeply. *Samadhi* is at your hand. Lie down in a flat posture. Keep your attention on the soul in atom point, take one or two breaths through the nostrils, only remain in atom point. Don't allow any thought to enter there. Breath will come out through mouth. Then inhale 1 or 2 times through the nostrils, and watch, watch and watch. Then you will get formless stage even *samadhi* stage.

You all take my deepest affection and enjoy blessings of God and Gurus.

Humble Hariharananda

From,
Swami H. Giri,
c/o. Dr. Gerald Peabody,
... Cloister Dr.
Rockville, MD 20852, USA.

My affectionate and divine Triloki Baba !

I am extremely happy to receive the Chandi and Hindu Puja Rahasya books.

You are the only Yogi who really meditates deeply and you are the only disciple who has real love for Gurus. You are the only disciple who has studied all authentic scriptures and memorized and stored in the brain. You are the only disciple who wants better realization and wants to get *samadhi*.

You can show my letter to my divine mother of the Samaj and inform my deepest regard to her and to reverend Sj. Radhanath Baba.

My eye operation was not completely successful. 23 days past but I cannot see a single letter. So treatment is going on. When my eye will be better then I will go to India.

Inform Chaturbhuj father and to all when I will go to Cuttack. I will remain in his house. I received the medicine.

I am writing this letter with right eye.

Meditate deeply and in your every action in practical life feel that the power of God is doing all works through your body. So you are the living power of God. Please feel it constantly.

I cannot write more. Pranams to all. ...

... Be bold, everything will be all right.

Humble H. Giri

Please send all letters to the proper persons.

To,
Triloki Dash, Lecturer,
Nua Sahi, Jobra,
Cuttack-3, Orissa.

My affectionate and divine Triloki Baba!

I am extremely happy to receive your divine letter, only true seeker like you who wants the company of Guru, can feel, without Gurus guidance makes the disciples far away from being realised. Meditate deeply, always feel Harihari ananda is within you and you are living power of God. Constantly think of Him before after and while performing action. As the ship is in the fierce winds and a little helm can save the ship, so every human being should keep one helm on God. Then no 49 types of air can disturb the *sadhaka*. Meditate very deeply and try your utmost not to marry. ...

I am well. I want to bow you all.

Eye is all right, maybe left eye may be operated.

Humble H. Giri

From,
H. Giri

To,
Triloki Dash

My affectionate and divine Triloki Baba!

I read your letter and I always remain with you. I have written one letter to Udaynath Baba, you can give it to the magazine (the letter written to Udaynath Baba by Gurudev). You will get my guidance through my letter, you all take my deepest affection and blessings.

Humble Hariharananda

Triloki Baba!

Take my deepest love, affection, regard and pranams. I write you many times with mind's pen. Inform my blessings to your friend who is newly married. Meditate and watch living presence of God in you and love Him.

Blessings for all. Inform Anita Ma my affection and blessing.

H. Giri

Prana priya[1] Triloki Baba!

I reached safely in the extreme cold and windy New York City. I am well. If I think of you I get divine joy. You are a true seeker and from the core of your heart you served me wholeheartedly. Surely you will get God realisation. The letter which I wrote to GOPALJE, you read it and make photocopy and send one copy to Rourkela, one in Sambalpur one for Yogeswarananda for publication in magazine. Meditate and watch Him in your every work.

You all take my deepest blessings.

Humble H. Giri

1 *prana priya*: dearer than life itself.

From,
H. Giri

11th April

My affectionate and divine father Triloki Baba!

... Now I say if you want to come to U.S.A. (if you have desire) then make passport and try to come in Puja vacation, because to get passport takes time. ...

So just after we can not make an other program.

I also tell, you got 4th Kriya more then two years so you are entitled to initiate. If you come here you are to initiate because many people will take initiation. ...

Please prepare. You are son of Brahmin. You are *brahmajna* (knower of Brahman). *ayam atma brahma. prajnanam brahma. sarva khalvidam brahma.*[1]

See the Bhagavad Gita, 14th chapter 5th verse. The whole body of each human being is Brahma the power of God but "*maya, moha, bhranti*"[2] and extrovert nature is so powerful it is why "*dasa chakre bhgavan bhut*"[3], only if you bow two times then you will be free from all things even body sense and you will feel the life movement sensation in the whole body universe. Then you will feel you are not body, some life movement sensation in the whole universe. This is "*sarva kalvidam brahma*."

Practice makes a man perfect. Only it requires extreme desire to make you free.

chatur je mina seyi ta jane ma jal theke je mukti achhe
tayi jele jakhan jal phelese lukay jele r ayer kacche
jal ediye tai se banche ma.
tayi ma ami nilam saran tora duti ranga charan
ediye gelo mayar bandhan mator ranga charan peye.

So look before you leap.

Patha bhranta hole pacharive se patha sadhujane. (If you miss the way in your journey, ask to one who knows the way.)

Oh how *maya* is so great! Wherever you look you will see
maya, maya, maya, moha, moha, moha, bhranti, bhranti.

Truth is very near in your whole body but truth will not come back. It is covered by untruth.

...

Be very careful

Humble Hariharananda

---

1 These are the few *mahavakyas* (great commandments) from the Upanishada. The meaning of these sentences are, 'This Soul is Brahman. Wisdom is Brahman. Everything is Brahman alone. I am Brahman.'

2 Delusion, illusion and error leading to suffering.

3 A Bengali Proverb, which means, people try to establish untruth as truth.

From, H. Giri

To, Triloki Das

Triloki Das, Naya sahi. Jobra. Cuttack- 3 Orissa

My One Soul!

I am extremely happy to receive your letter. I am improving but I am getting wrinkles in the face, hand, arms, almost baldheaded.

I wrote you many letters, articles, please read them and correct them. ...

... You are the real person who want God realization, and are meditating deeply and regularly with love.

Your whole body is the body of God "*aham ima tisra devata*." In you, there are three, creator, preserver and destroyer. Gross, astral and causal. ***Jagannath, Shubhadra*** and ***Balabhadra***. This is "*tisra devata*" (A+U+M = OM).

In your every disposition you are getting three steps. As an example, Creation of appetite, preservation of appetite (so long you are eating food) and destruction of your appetite (means satisfaction of appetite). So watch Him always in your every action. God is constantly evolving you in three steps. So watch him in your practical life and during the time of meditation perceive "*trayam ekatra samyama,*[1] *dharana, dhyana samadhi*"

The moment you will bow once you are completely free from everything. This is *pratyahara*. You are only realizing the movement sensation of loving power of God in your whole system. Even you are not feeling "*na sthanam na manam*." "*nada vindu kalatitam*", but you will not feel your existence. That is your perception of nothingness. That is called *prajnanam brahma*. That is your pulse less stage "*atmavid atmaiva bhava*" (Oneness with the Soul).

Try to get that stage.

In your practical life you always feel you are the living power of God. All the time feel you are Soul only.

Blessings of God and Gurus. You are the top most person who has strong idea of the Vedas, the Upanisadas, the Gita, the Chandi, even

Patanjali's Yoga Sutra and some other authentic spiritual books.
I bow you all.

Humble servant

Hariharananda

1 Please see the Yoga Sutra of Patanjali III/4.

From,
H. Giri written by Claudia Ma

To,
Triloki Dash

April 20th 93

My respected and divine world teacher,

You are loved and honoured by everybody.
Everybody tells that you are the next descendant of H. Giri. He loves you very much.
Babaji is not feeling well. He cannot write. He cannot see and read well and has pain in the neck, even there is a little swelling there.
It is not possible for Babaji to sit for a longer period. He has pain in the whole right side of the body, even in the right arm. So that's why he cannot answer all of your letters.
There's not anything why Babaji should be unhappy, angry of dissatisfied with you. Only because of his difficult bodily condition he could not write to you sooner.
Babaji will fly from New York to India and will reach Calcutta towards 29th or 30th of May. He will stay there at Debi Baba's house.I'm giving my extreme regards and pranam to you and to everybody at that place.

Claudia Ma

My affectionate and divine father of my prior birth, Triloki Baba!
I am not at all unhappy with you. I am extremely unwell.
My affection, regard, love and pranams to you all.

Humble Hariharananda

Triloki Dash,
Karar Ashram, Swargadwar,
Puri, Orissa.

My affectionate and divine Triloki Baba!

Your letter gave me extreme joy. God is at your hand, so meditate and watch Him in your every thought and work.

sman śabde śavam prokta śānam śayānam ucyate.[1] *Sman* means dead body *śānam* means *soi kari achhi* (Remaining as if sleeping).

The living life of God is lying in the dead body. It is why every dead body is *sman* and *śānam* means the living power of God is hiding in every human body. So every human body is *smashana*. It is written in Anhika Kritya book written by Shyamacharan Deva Sharma.

Blessing for all.

Humble H. Giri

1 A verse from the scriptures describing the inner meaning of the body as the cremation ground.

Perchtoldsdorf, Austria

14.8.93

Triloki Dash
AT/Po. Nimpur
Jagatpur, Orissa
India

My affectionate and divine Triloki Baba, father of my prior birth.

I am extremely happy to receive your heart touching letter.

Our ticket of Rourkela is booked for 6th. I will remain there up to 10.Feb.94 ... ...

Then I will go Jharsuguda, Sambalpur Bhawanipatna. Then in beginning of March I will go to Jagatpur, Cuttack, on 18th morning March. One hour in 173 Cuttack Rd, Bhubaneshwar, then Puri up to 23rd March then on 24th March 94 Calcutta. Then 7th of April 94, Holland, Switzerland, Germany, Austria then back to India.

I am well. My back pain is very less. I am writing in lying posture.

Meditate very deeply. Keep 1% breath in the fontanel ... ... you are not watching in the whole passage of nostril up to the top. Only remain on the top with the Almighty Father who is inhaling from above. Even you are not watching the breath. Then you will feel

"*na sthanam, na manam, na ca nada vindum, na rupan, na rekha, nacha dhatu varnam nada vindu kalatitam.*"[1]

Breath will remain on the top. As if 99% no breath. No more movement sensation, no light, only a very feeble sound, as if you are on the stage of *samadhi* pulselessness stage.

Try, try and try, and get *nirvikalpa samadhi*. Give my love to Suman Bramachari.

dhairya yasya pitā kṣamā ca janani śānti chira gehinī
satyam ca suta dayā ca bhaginī bhrātaḥ manḥ samyama
sayyā bhūmitala diśo 'pi vasanam jñānāmṛtam bhojanam
yasya ete kutumbinaḥ vada sakhe, bhayam kasmāt yoginaḥ.[2]

You all are my better Gurus. I bow you all,
Humbly H. Giri

I am glad to know that many are coming in Bhubaneshwar for meditation.

(On 18th March, I can stay in the house of Vidya Sagar Baba in the evening you can come and I will conduct class and on 19th morning I can go to Puri. Arrange, Give to the news paper) ...

Humbly H. Giri

---

1 This is a quotation from the *Niranjanastakam Stotra*, which narrates the state of deep mediation, meaning, " no knowledge of the place, no body sense, no sound, no light, beyond all experiences, absorbed in the formless stage."

2 The Yogi who has patience as the father, forgiveness as the mother, eternal peace as the consort, truthfulness as the brother, compassion as the sister, mind-control as the brother, whose bed is the earth, whose clothes are the infinity of space, and whose food is the nectar of knowledge, oh my friend, tell me where is the cause of fear? *Vairagya Satakam* of *Bhartruhari*.

To,
Triloki Dash, Lecturer,
Karar Ashram, Swargadwar Rd.
Puri, Orissa.

My One Soul!

The moment I saw your name in your letter, my whole body became more divine and more joy. Meditate deeply and remain in *vicharani samadhi* stage.[1] Feel that you are living power of God; watch Him constantly. Remain calmly active and actively calm. Inform my affection to Yogeswarananda Baba.

You all take my blessings. End of November, Puri.

Blessings.

Humble. H. Giri

---

1 There are seven stages of *samadhi*, as described in yogic scriptures, out of which the third one is *vicharani samadhi*, meaning to be absorbed in God-consciousness even in normal activities of life.

From,
H. Giri

To,
Triloki Das
Nua Sahi, Jobra,
Cuttack 3, Orissa.

I read your letters. I write you daily. Even through letters, *yogasiddha sannidhya matrena yogasiddhim bhavati.*[1] *praner prati chanchlata i yajna.* are of 4 types, 1. *bhautika samsthiti* 2. *karmika samsthiti* 3. *atmika samsthiti* 4. *avyakta samsthiti.*

From formless the inaudible talk is coming in 3rd place in the soul. Suppose the Lord is giving you hunger, which you perceive in the body. This is *atmika samsthiti*. Then (2nd) you are asking for food, which is in your front. Then *karmika samsthiti*, you are offering oblation in the *vaiśvanara* fire (3rd fire) *vaiśvanara agnaye svāhā idam te na mama.*

Although you are eating, yet you are not eating, you are remaining compassionately detached.

In this way in the practically doing works, you are not married you are not enjoying sexually still you are telling God, *tvayā niyojitā yajne tvayā tvam hi prapujitā.*

This is meditation plus right action, but when you will meditate then surely you will feel you have no physical existence. You do not know where you are sitting. You do not know where is your body. You will only feel from somewhere it is moving. You will extremely love Him, because you are watching everywhere the power of God is moving (U) and you are hearing many types of sound (A) and many types of light (M).

Even then you will try to get *nirvikalpa samadhi* means *nada vindu kalatitam*, means you are merged in the self. ...

You all take my affection, oneness and my pranams. You all are more powerful if you all meditate then surely you will feel it.

Blessings of God and Gurus.

Humble Hariharananda.

---

1 The company of the realized one, accelerates spiritual evolution.

2 All vibration in the *prana* (life energy) is a *yajna*, or sacrifice.

From,
H. Giri
c/p Sj. D.P. Chatterjee, Advocate,
... Hazra Road, Calcutta.

26.3.1994

To
Triloki Das

My Soul,

I read many letters, but you did not give me the address of Angul. Even you did not give me pin code.

I am and I was in Puri always. My health did not permit to go. Because in the moment I will be in the gate many will stand to bow me. Apart from this I cannot sit near Shriyukteshwar temple, or in the hall, or in the meeting place, nor I can talk.

So, if I would go to Puri, it will be extreme strain on me.

I am always with you. I heard from many persons that your talk was highly accepted by the mass people. I pray to God that you will be highly realized.

Watch him always in the fontanel. Remain alert and watch that your whole body is the body of God, this is *bha-ga-va* that is *te-va-su* that is also *de-va-ya*. So you always watch that your skin, flesh, blood, breath is the life and your body is the body of God.

I am unwell. So I do not want any one to come to me.

You all are my God. I want to bow you all.

Humble Hariharananda

From,
Swami H. Giri,
c/o. Sj. D. P. Chatterjee, Advocate,
... Hazra Rd.
Calcutta-700026, India.

To,
Brah. Triloki Baba,
c/o. Dr. Peter Bäurle,
Beheimgasse 44,
A- 1170 Wien, Vienna, Europe.

23-01-95

My affectionate and divine Triloki Baba!

I am extremely happy to receive your very sweet , divine and humble letter. Please maintain it.

Please read Upanishad before you are talking. Then you can say every day new.

I pray for you so that you will be a world teacher. Remain as long you can, and talk and act like Hariharananda, then you will be loved by all ...

... Always watch your negative, read every day the Gita 4th chapter last Verse and also 13th chapter 8th to 11th Verse. ...

... All the time seek Him through breath.

I bow you all.

Humble Hariharananda

From,
Swami H. Giri,
c/o. Sj. D.P. Chatterje, Advocate,
... Hazra Road,
Calcutta-700026.

To,
Brah. Triloki Baba,
c/o. Dr. Peter Bäurle,
Beheimgasse 44,
1170 Vienna, Austria, Europe.

Brahmachari Triloki Baba!

I read your lovely letters. I am happy that you are meditating deeply and silently you are doing work and the people of Europe they feel that you are vastly learned in Sanskrit, also you have gone through so many authentic religious books, the Vedas, the Upanisadas, the Brahmasutra, the Bhagavad Gita, the Chandi, the Bible, the Koran, the Torah and many other Samhitas which is not read even by many religious men.

It is my desire that you should stay permanently in Europe, even you can go to America and India only for 3 months. You are fortunate that within a short period you got Green Card of Austria. So you should stay as a Vice President of Vienna Ashram. I am President and after my death you will be President. ...

... Please keep this letter with you. Now you show this letter to Christine mother and Dr. Peter Bäurle. That after my death you will be the President. You all take my deepest affection and blessings. I am improving quickly. Maybe on 12th May I will go to Europe. Cut the above letter and store carefully.

Humble Hariharananda H. Giri

From,
Swami H. Giri,
c/o. Sj. D. P. Chatterjee, Advocate,
... Hazra Rd. Calcutta-700026.
To,
Christine Jacobsen,
c/o. Dr. Peter Bäurle,
Beheimgasse 44,
1170 Wien, Vienna, Europe.

6.2.95

My affectionate, pure, perfect, divine and holy loving mother Christine Ma!

Your tears (flow holy love) for Guru, still makes me more holy and Godly. You arc uncommon divine mother.

As one moon is enough to remove the darkness of the night so one Christine mother is enough to establish Authentic Kriya Yoga Center in Vienna.

I am improving quickly. At present I am taking meditation class, also I am initiating people.

I told ... ... that I will go to Hamburg on 12th May direct from India and you will help me to take there. I will stay a few days in Hamburg.

Now I am telling I am President and Brahmachari Triloki Baba is the Vice President ... ... After my death Brahmachari Triloki Baba will be President.

1) Triloki Baba is a Brahmachari and he did not marry.
2) Triloki Baba is well versed in Sanskrit and hc has completed the studies of the Vedas, the Upanisadas, the Brahmasutra, the Yoga Sutra of Patanjali, all Samhitas, the Bhagavad Gita, the Koran, the Torah, the Bible and many other authentic spiritual books for God-realisation, and no one of my Acharyas are well versed like him. Even I some times consult with Triloki Baba about the spiritual studies. Even I learn something from him.
3) Triloki Baba is highly qualified.
4) Triloki Baba has self restraint. He talks very less and he has almost no

negative in him.
5) Before the birth of Triloki Baba one Yogi came and told that his son will be world teacher so you should keep his name Triloki.
6) Triloki Baba does not take even tea and coffee and from his boyhood he is taking very simple food and no rich food. Triloki Baba can sing song and can speak sweetly and humbly.
7) Triloki Baba can talk in 5 languages. Even he is learning German language and French language. He will talk in German language within one year.
8) Triloki Baba has started one Ashram in Jagatpur, Cuttack, Orissa, with his own income.
9) Triloki Baba is the Govt. Professor he is still in his service.
10) Triloki Baba will leave this service and will stay in Europe nine months in a year and he will spread the authentic Kriya Yoga technique in Europe and all over the world.
So Triloki Baba will be the President after my demise. Please do not destroy my letter and read among Board members.

I bow to everybody,

Humble Hariharananda

24. In front of Samadhi Temple of Shriyukteshwar

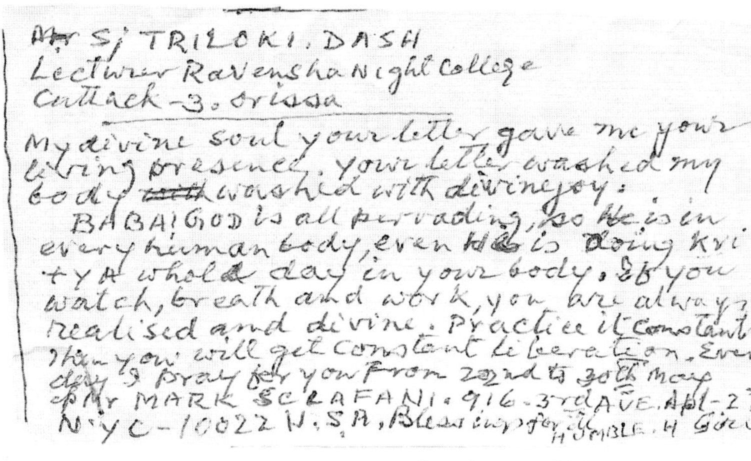

Mr Sj TRILOKI. DASH
Lecturer Ravensha Night College
Cuttack-3. Orissa
My divine soul your letter gave me your living presence. your letter washed my body ~~with~~ washed with divinejoy:
BABA! GOD is all pervading, so He is in every human body, even He is doing Kriya whole day in your body. If you watch, breath and work, you are always realised and divine. Practice it constantly then you will get constant liberation. Every day I pray for you from 22nd to 30th may c/o Mr MARK SCLAFANI. 916-3rd AVE. Apt-2D NYC-10022 U.S.A, Blessings for all HUMBLE. H Giri

1. The soul-stirring first letter, 1986

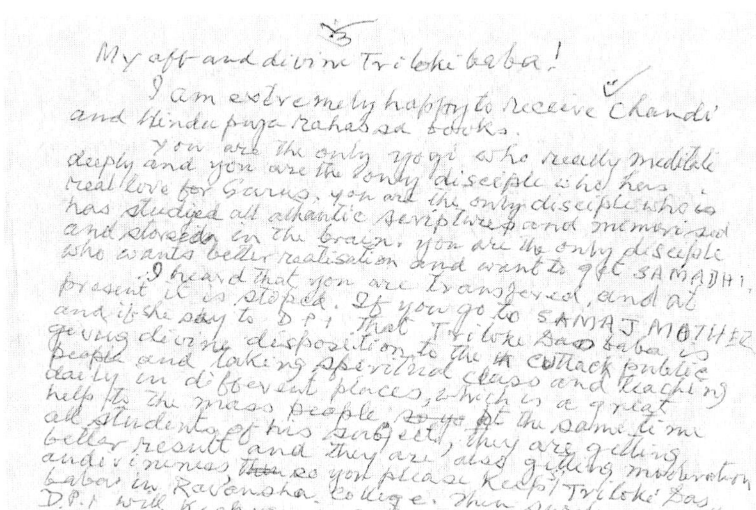

My aff and divine Triloki baba!
I am extremely happy to receive Chandi and Hindu puja rahasya books.
You are the only yogi who really meditate deeply and you are the only disciple who has real love for Gurus. you are the only disciple who has studied all authentic scriptures and memorised and stored in the brain. you are the only disciple who wants better realisation and want to get SAMADHI.
I heard that you are transferred, and at present it is stoped. If you go to SAMAJ MOTHER and if she say to D.P.I that Triloki Das baba is giving divine disposition to the Cuttack public people and taking spiritual class and teaching daily in different places, which is a great help to the mass people, at the same time all students of his subject, they are getting better result and they are also getting motivation and divineness, so you please keep Sj Triloki Das baba in Ravensha college. Then surely you D.P.I will keep you in Cuttack.
You can show my letter to my divine mother of SAMAJ and inform my deepest regard to her and to Reverend Sj Radhanath baba.
My eye operation was not completely successful. 23 days past but I can not see a single letter. So treatment is going on.

2. Transmitting his care and love

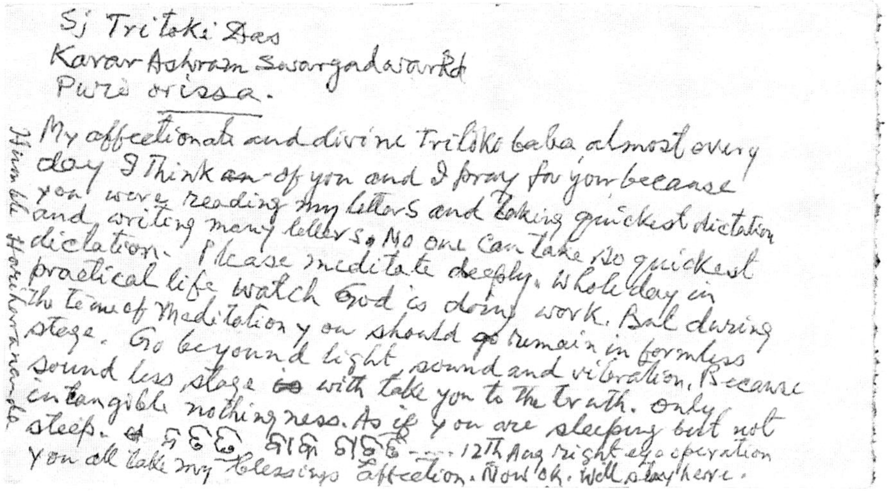

Sj Triloki Das
Karar Ashram Swargadwar Rd
Puri Orissa.

My affectionate and divine Triloki baba almost every day I Think ~~on~~ of you and I pray for you because you were reading my letters and taking quickest dictation and writing many letters. No one can take so quickest dictation. Please meditate deeply. Whole day in practical life watch God is doing work. But during the time of Meditation you should ~~go~~ remain in formless stage. Go beyound light, sound and vibration. Because sound less stage ~~is~~ with take you to the truth. only intangible nothingness. As if you are sleeping but not sleep. [illegible] ---- 12th Aug right eye operation You all take my blessings affection. Now ok. Well stay here.

Humble Harihrananda

3. You are in my daily thoughts

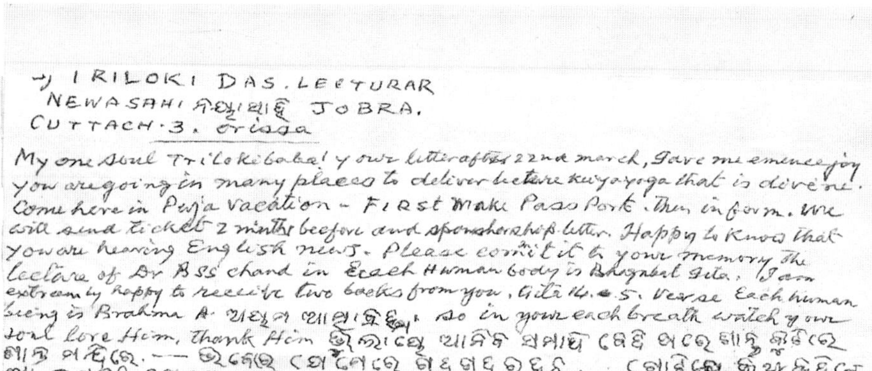

Sj TRILOKI DAS. LECTURAR
NEWASAHI [illegible] JOBRA.
CUTTACH-3. Orissa

My one soul Trilokibaba! your letter after 22nd march, Gave me emence joy you are going in many places to deliver lecture kriyayoga that is divine. Come here in Puja vacation - FIRST Make Pass Port. Then inform. We will send ticket 2 months beefore and sponsorship letter. Happy to know that you are hearing English news. Please commit it to your memory the lecture of Dr BSS chand in Each Human body is Bhagabat Gita. I am extreamly happy to receive two books from you, Gita 14.5. Verse Each human being is Brahma A [illegible]. so in your each breath watch your soul love Him, thank Him [illegible]. I am always with in you. Humble. Harinanda,

4. His encouragement, 1988

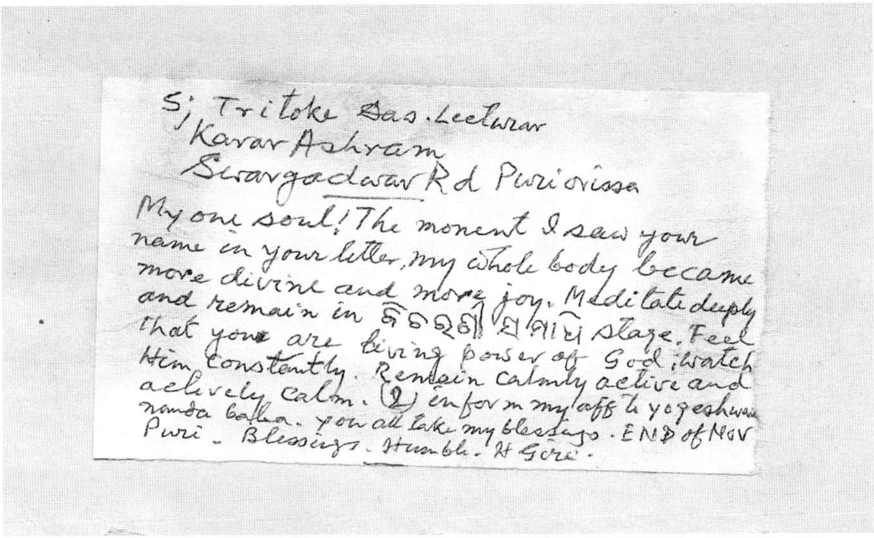

S; Tritoke Das. Lecturar
Karar Ashram
Swargadwar Rd Puri orissa
My one soul! The moment I saw your
name in your letter, my whole body became
more divine and more joy. Meditate deeply
and remain in [illegible] stage. Feel
that you are living power of God; watch
Him constantly. Remain calmly active and
actively calm. (2) inform my aff to yogeshwar
nanda baba. you all take my blessings. END of NOV
Puri - Blessings - Humble. H Giri.

5. Your letter gives divinity, 1986

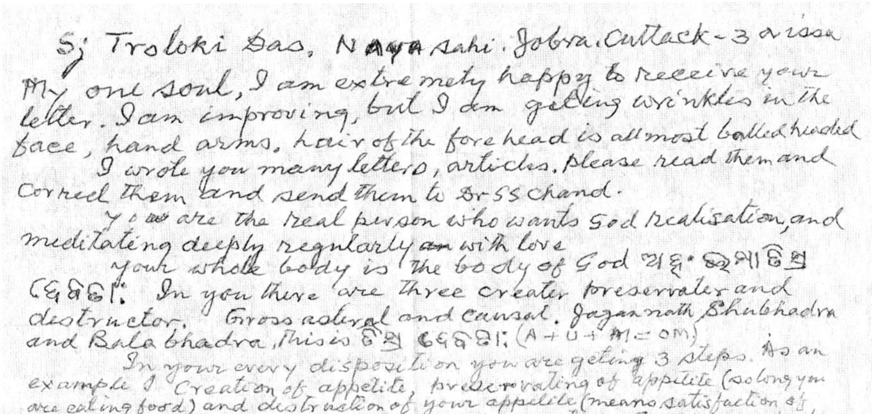

S; Troloki Das, Naya sahi. Jobra. Cuttack - 3 orissa
My one soul, I am extremely happy to receive your
letter. I am improving, but I am geting wrinkles in the
face, hand arms. hair of the fore head is allmost balled headed
I wrote you many letters, articles. please read them and
Correct them and send them to Dr SS chand.
You are the real person who wants God realisation, and
meditateing deeply regularly ~~an~~ with love
your whole body is the body of God [illegible]
[illegible]. In you there are three creater preservater and
destructor. Gross asteral and Causal. Jagannath, Shubhadra
and Balabhadra, This is [illegible] (A + U + M = OM)
In your every disposition you are geting 3 steps. As an
example I Creation of appetite, preservating of appitite (so long you
are eating food) and destruction of your appetite (means satisfaction of
appetite. So watch him always in your every action. God is constantly
evolveing you with three steps. So watch him in your practical life but

6. Practical instructions

Sj Triloke Das. NUASAHI JOBRA. Cuttack-3. Orissa.
I read your 3 letters. I write you daily. Even through letters [illegible]
[illegible]
[illegible]
[illegible]
[illegible]
(4) [illegible] From formless, the inaudible talk is coming in 3rd place in the soul, suppose Lord is giving you hungal, which you perceive it in the body. This is [illegible] (2nd) Then you are asking for food, which is in your front. Then [illegible] you are offering oblation in the [illegible] fire (3rd fire) [illegible]
Although you are eating yet you are not eating you are remaining compassionately detatched.
In this way in the practically doing works you are not married you are not enjoying sexually still you are letting God [illegible]
This is meditation plus right action but when you will meditate then surely you will feel you have no phycical existence, you do not know where you are siting. You do not know where is your body you will only feel some extremely vibration, because where it is moving you will where the power of God is moving and your are hearing many types of sound and many types of light (M)
Even then you will try to get [illegible] means you are merged in the self.
I am well. Tell the son of Lingaraj baba to study LAW. His father can train him. Then within 2 years time he may be married, and he will be very good lawyer. Because his father is Justice high court So

7. Scriptural discussion

[illegible] I reached safely in the extreme cold and windy New york city. I am well. If I think of you I get divine joy you are a true seeker and from the core of your heart you [illegible] me wholeheartedly. Surely you will get God realization. The letter which I wrote to GOPALJE, you read it and make xerox and send one copy to Rourkela, one in Sambalpur one for yogeswara nanda for publication in magazine. Meditate and [illegible] in your every works you all take my deepest blessings. [illegible]

8. His assurance

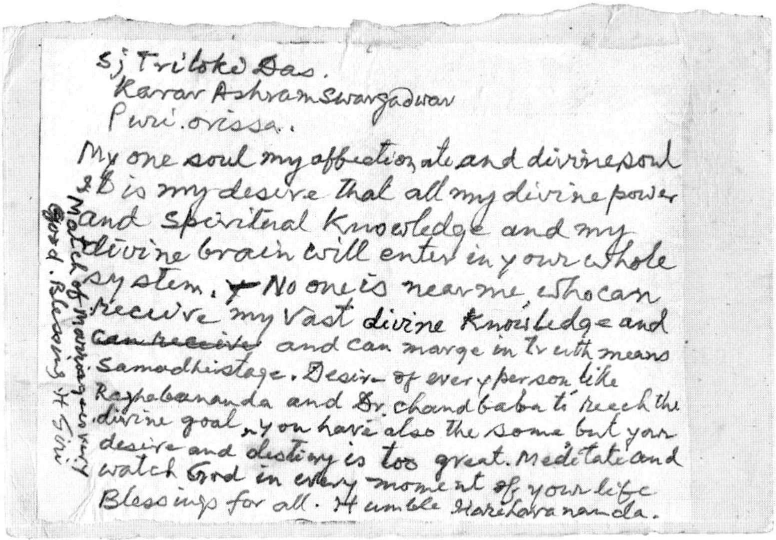

Sj Triloki Das.
Karar Ashram Swargadwar
Puri. orissa.
My one soul my affectionate and divine soul
It is my desire that all my divine power
and spiritual knowledge and my
divine brain will enter in your whole
system. No one is near me who can
receive my vast divine knowledge and
~~can receive~~ and can marge in truth means
Samadhistage. Desire of every person like
Raghabananda and Dr. chandbaba to reech the
divine goal, you have also the some but your
desire and destiny is too great. Meditate and
watch God in every moment of your life
Blessings for all. Humble Hariharananda.

Match of marriage is very good. Blessing H Giri

9. His trust

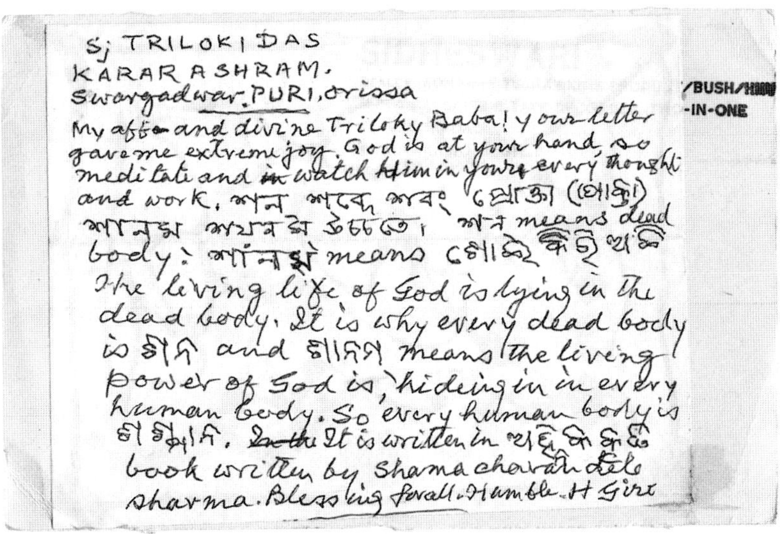

Sj TRILOKI DAS
KARAR ASHRAM.
Swargadwar. PURI, orissa
My affe and divine Triloky Baba! your letter
gave me extreme joy. God is at your hand, so
meditate and ~~in~~ watch ~~Him~~ in your every thought
and work. [illegible] ([illegible])
[illegible] [illegible] means dead
body: [illegible] means [illegible]
The living life of God is lying in the
dead body. It is why every dead body
is [illegible] and [illegible] means the living
power of God is, hideing in in every
human body. So every human body is
[illegible]. ~~In the~~ It is written in [illegible]
book written by Shama charan Lele
sharma. Blessing for all. Humble. H Giri

10. God is at your hand

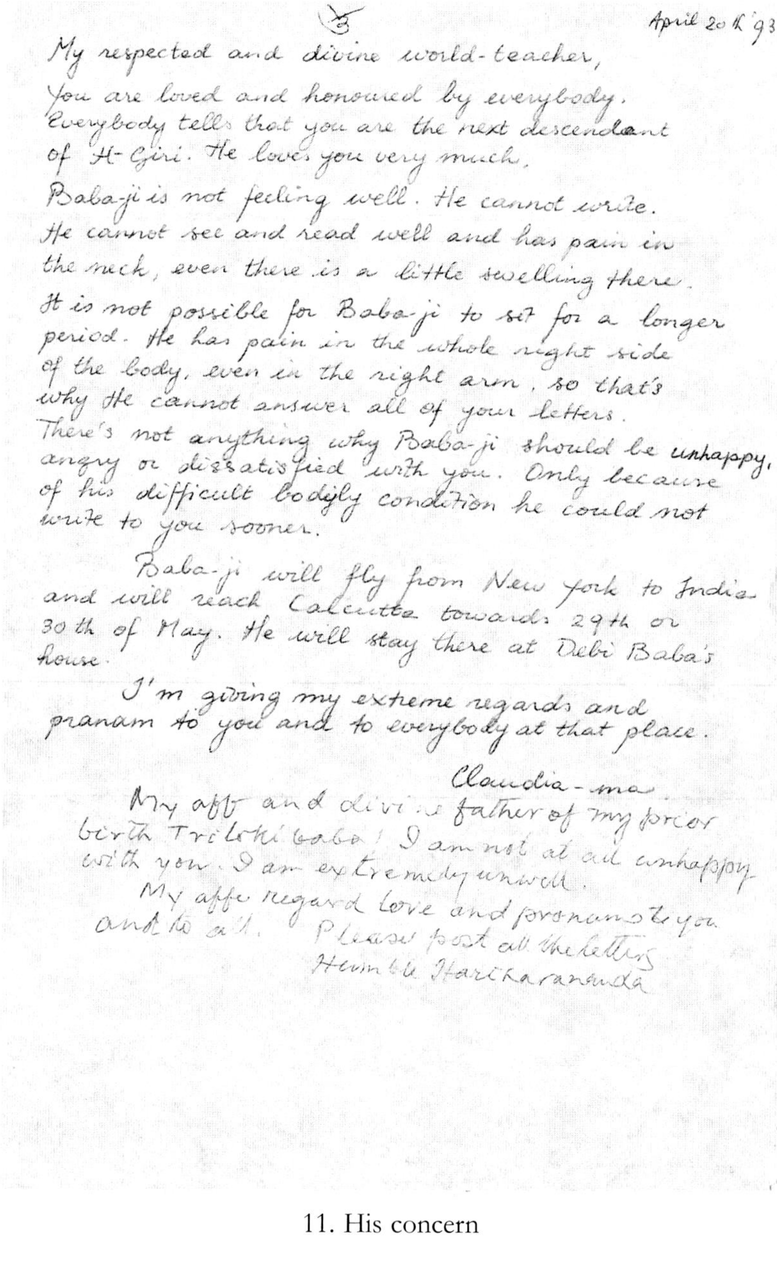

April 20th '93

My respected and divine world-teacher,
You are loved and honoured by everybody.
Everybody tells that you are the next descendant
of H-Giri. He loves you very much.
Baba-ji is not feeling well. He cannot write.
He cannot see and read well and has pain in
the neck, even there is a little swelling there.
It is not possible for Baba-ji to sit for a longer
period. He has pain in the whole right side
of the body, even in the right arm, so that's
why He cannot answer all of your letters.
There's not anything why Baba-ji should be unhappy,
angry or dissatisfied with you. Only because
of his difficult bodyly condition he could not
write to you sooner.

Baba-ji will fly from New York to India
and will reach Calcutta towards 29th or
30th of May. He will stay there at Debi Baba's
house.

I'm giving my extreme regards and
pranam to you and to everybody at that place.

Claudia-ma.

My aff and divine father of my prior
birth Trilokibaba! I am not at all unhappy
with you. I am extremely unwell.
My affe regard love and pronams to you
and to all. Please post all the letters
Humble Hariharananda

11. His concern

(1) First you read this letter 26th feb 91

My aff and divine Triloke baba!

I ~~w~~ received your 3 divine letters which is heart touching sweet and divine.

You are the only real seeker of God. and you have studied Upanisad Patanjoly, Bhagabad Gita Brahmasutra even many spiritual authentic books. and no one except you. So in your life you must get nir bikalpa समाधि. only it depends on greatest desire, your whole life will be peaceful and wealthy.

Any word or letter I am writing, I am watching the power of God is writing through my hand and I am feeling divine joy. So you read my letter and watch that living power of God is reading letter through your soul. This is soul culture.

So long you will not marry marry you can get constant alert ness. In this way you you can avoid marriage, your spiritual foundation will be very strong. In every letter I am writing I am geting divine ness! who is writing? dead body? or two bodies. So when divine body is the ~~soul a~~ sole doer then why should we forget Him. Try Try Try constantly.

You are pure sweet kind loving generous, broad-minded. This is the sign of a GURU. See Gita 2nd ch 54 verse then up to the end.

Baba whether your mother got the new set of teeth? Please do it. It is my desire to pay for it. she is my own mother and father I regard them because they are your parents.

Baba! I wrote one letter on 8th feb. I did not post it because I thought I will go to India in the begining of march ~~but I am~~ it is why I did not post it. Now I am sure I will not go due to my eye operation. Even my prostate trouble is so strong at any moment I am to go to the hospital. the doctors are so good, it is why I ~~am~~ will not go I will stay. c/o Dr G Peabody. 4904. CLOISTER. Dr Rock Ville. MARY Land 20852. USA. Tel:- 301. 564. 5724

I humbly request you please give it to all news paper that Eye of Swami Hariharananda Giri will be operated in April ~~also before~~ so in this year he will not be in Puri annual function on 22nd March 91

If you dont give then many people will think I am bad man I am not Guru. Guru should inform us – why ~~we~~ we will not see him we all are coming to see Guru.

So you must give it to the news paper. Please think deeply and do it

You please go to the house of Gold smith baba to guide them. You will always get my guidence from the distant Hariharananda is always siting in the whole body of Triloke Baba.

You all take my deepest affection and enjoy blessing of God and Gurus.

Humble Hariharananda

PS. Please hear English news of Calcutta or Delhi and correct your pronounciation. Keep it in a note book. and correct.

Humble Hariharananda

12. Signs of the Guru

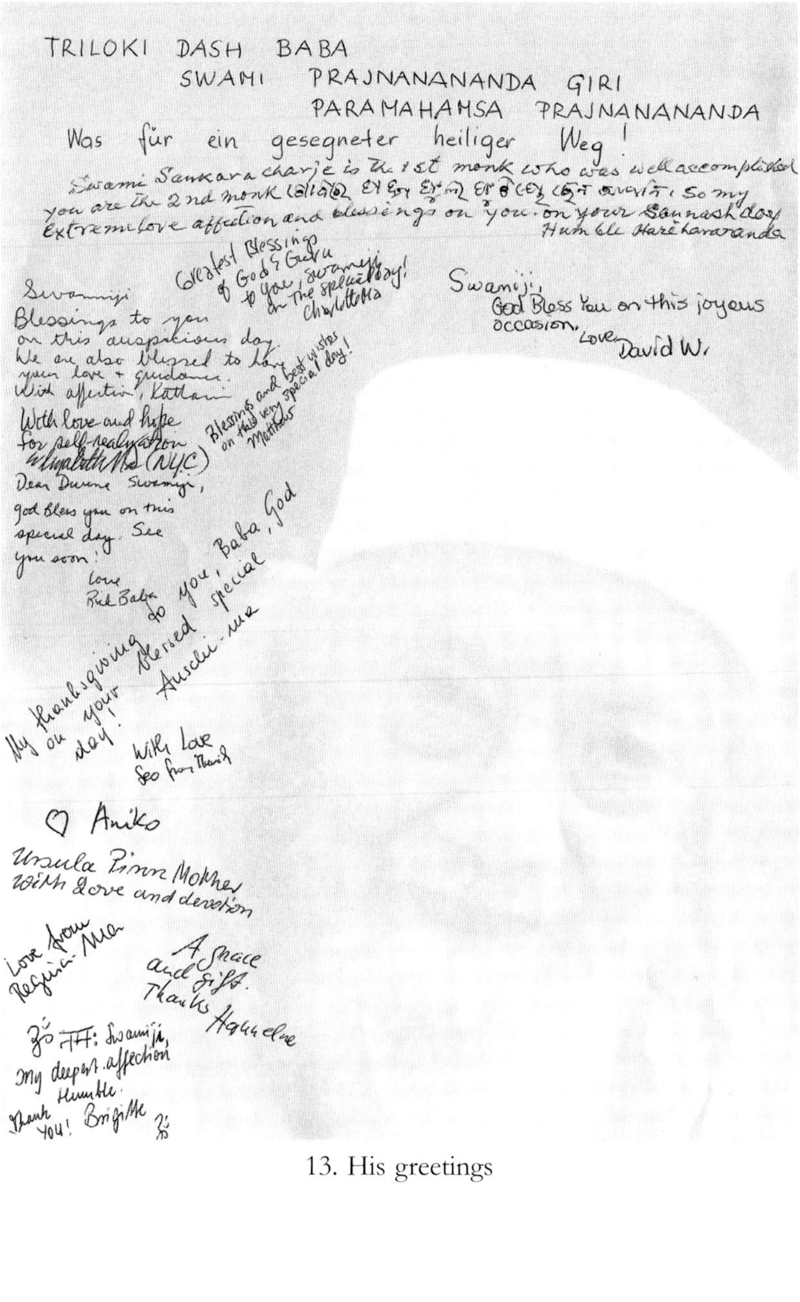

TRILOKI DASH BABA
SWAMI PRAJNANANANDA GIRI
PARAMAHAMSA PRAJNANANANDA
Was für ein gesegneter heiliger Weg!
Swami Sankaracharje is the 1st monk who was well accomplished
you are the 2nd monk [illegible] So my
Extreme love affection and blessings on you. on your Sannash day
Humble Hariharananda

Greatest Blessings
of God & Guru
to you, Swamiji
on the special day!
Charlotte Ma

Swamiji,
God Bless You on this joyous
occasion.
Love David W.

Swamiji
Blessings to you
on this auspicious day.
We are also blessed to have
your love + guidance.
With affection, Kathan

Blessings and best wishes
on this very special day!
Matthäus

With love and hope
for self-realization
[illegible] (NYC)

Dear Divine Swamiji,
God Bless you on this
special day. See
you soon!
Love
Rick Baba

My thanksgiving to you, Baba, God
on your blessed special
day!
Auschi-ma

With Love
Seo from Thanh

♡ Aniko

Ursula Pinn Mother
With love and devotion

Love from
Regina-Ma

A grace
and gift.
Thanks Hannelore

ॐ [illegible]: Swamiji,
my deepest affection
Humble.
Thank YOU! Brigitte ॐ

13. His greetings

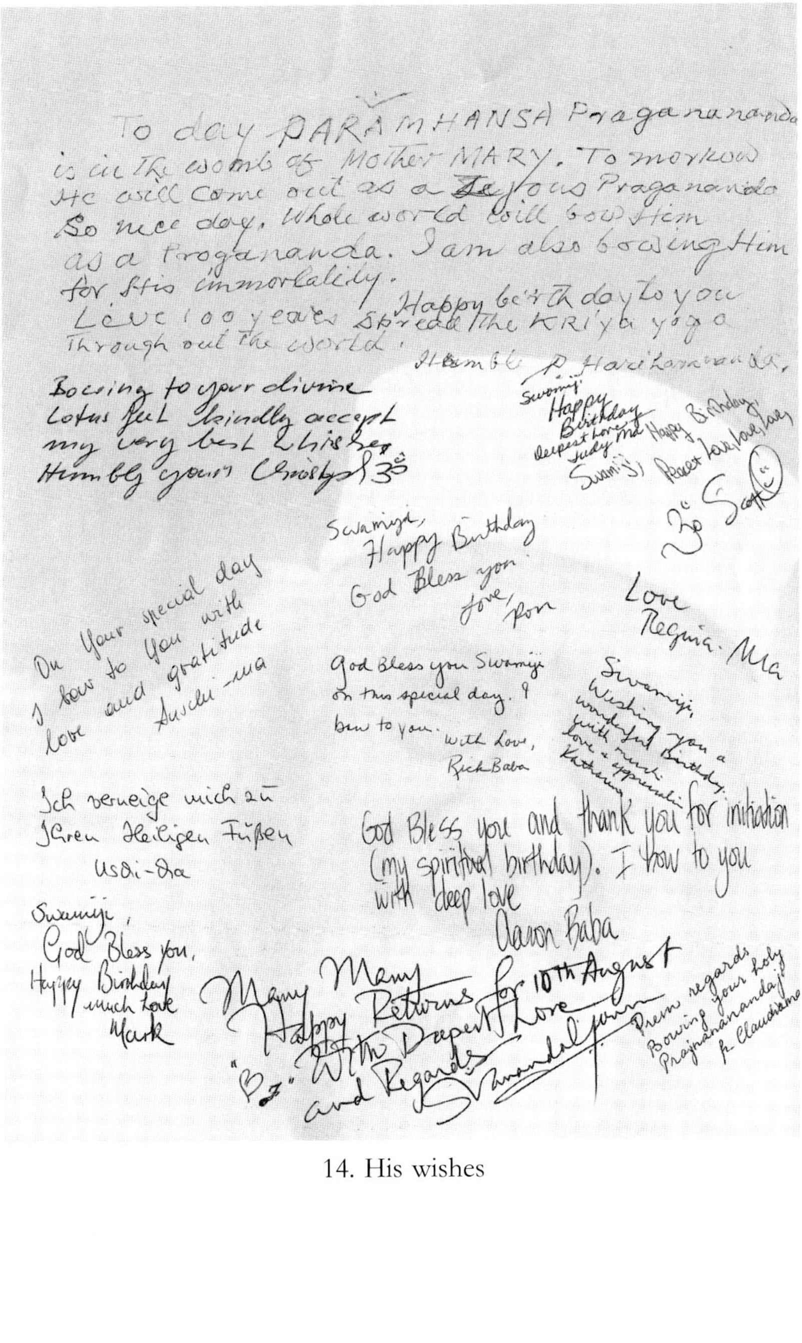
To day PARAMHANSA Praganananda
is in the womb of Mother MARY. To morrow
He will come out as a Jesus Praganananda
So nice day, Whole world will bow Him
as a Praganananda. I am also bowing Him
for His immortality.
Happy birth day to you
Live 100 years Spread the KRIYA yoga
Through out the world.
Humble P. Hariharananda.

Bowing to your divine
Lotus feet kindly accept
my very best wishes
Humbly yours Christopher 3

Swamiji
Happy
Birthday
Deepest Love
Judy Ma

Happy Birthday
Swamiji
Deepest love, love, love

ॐ Scott

Swamiji,
Happy Birthday
God Bless you
Love, Ron

Love
Regina Ma

On Your special day
I bow to You with
love and gratitude
Aurelie-ma

God Bless you Swamiji
on this special day. I
bow to you.
With Love,
Rick Baba

Swamiji,
Wishing you a
wonderful Birthday
with much
love & appreciation
Katherine

Ich verneige mich zu
Ihren Heiligen Füßen
Usdi-Ma

God Bless you and thank you for initiation
(my spiritual birthday). I bow to you
with deep love
Aaron Baba

Swamiji,
God Bless you,
Happy Birthday
much Love
Mark

Many Many
Happy Returns for 10th August
"BJ" With Deepest Love
and Regards
Swanandaji yours

Prem regards
Bowing your holy
Prajnanananda ji
fr. Claudia Ma

14. His wishes

25. Together in Vienna

Glossary of Sanskrit Words

abhisheka: annointment, offering a ceremonial bath with the chanting of specific *mantras*.

advaitabhava: *advaita* means non-dual, *bhava* attitude. The attitude of perceiving the omnipresent God.

ahavaniya agni: the name of the fire in the dorsal (heart) center.

alekh sampradaya: a religious group in Eastern India and especially in Orissa, who pray and worship the formless God. The wandering monks belonging to this order follow a strictly disciplined life.

artha: money; one of the four-fold objectives in Vedic culture, which represents material excellence.

ashram: monastery

baba: father, affectionate term for Guru.

Balabhadra: the elder brother of Krishna. One of the three presiding deities in the Jagannath Temple in Puri. Literally meaning omnipotent.

Bhartruhari: a poet and a king who later on became a renowned Yogi, the author of three classical texts in Sanskrit, *Vairagya Shatakam*, *Niti Shatakam* and *Shringar Shatakam*.

Bengali: a language usually spoken in Bengal, India and Bangladesh.

bhoo-samadhi: *bhoo* means earth, *samadhi* means to bury. It is a ritualistic way of burying the deceased body of a monk.

bhranti: mistakes, doubts.

brahmachari: one who observes the vow of a *brahmacharya*, which literally means celibacy and sense control and esoterically to roam (*char*) in God (*Brahman*), or to live in constant God-consciousness.

brahman: the formless God. Derived from the root *brih*, 'to grow' or 'to expand'.

brahmin: the first caste in the ancient Vedic social system of priests and teachers; metaphorically those who are on the spiritual path; to be in God (*Brahman*).

chackra: literally wheel or disc, a spiritual center-plexus in the spinalcolumn and brain. Derived from the root verb *char*, 'to move'.

darshan: holy vision or experience; the path of knowledge; philosophy.

deha: the body, literally that which can be burned.

dehi: the indwelling Self.

dharana: the art of concentration, one of the eight limbs of Yoga as described by Patanjali.

dhyana: meditation. The seventh limb of *Patanjali*'s *asthanga yoga* system.

Durga Puja: *Puja* means ritualistic worship. *Durga* is the Divine Mother, who removes all obstacles from human life, the consort of *Shiva*. The festival of *Durga Puja* is celebrated during autumn and spring.

Ganesh Puja: the worship of *Ganesha*, the elephant faced deity, Lord of Wisdom, remover of obstacles. This festival is usually celebrated in the month of August and September.

Gita, Bhagavad Gita: the Song of the Lord, part of the *Mahabharata*, consisting of eighteen chapters and seven hundred verses, composed by *Maharshi Vyasa*, a great seer.

go, goru: means cattle.

Guru Gita: is a holy book composed of a conversation held between *Shiva* and *Parvati* describing the glory of the Divine Masters.

Guru, Gurudeva: 'weigthy one', divine spiritual preceptor.

Guruvara: Thursday, the day dedicated to the Guru, the Masters, and the planet Jupiter.

hamsa: the material perishable body is *ham*. The power by which you inhale through your nose is *sa*, which means your own Soul. In the *hamsa* stage you forget your existence and only feel that *sa*, inhalation, is the life of the gross body.

havana paddhati: the ritualistic procedure for conducting a Vedic firc ceremony.

Hindi: one of the main languages in India, considered as the national language.

ishta mantra: a special *mantra* given by the teacher to the student, according to his/her personal deity.

jagrad samadhi: a state of inner awakening, when one experiences the blissful state of Divine Communion while in the wakeful, active state.

jala samadhi: *jala* means water. The ceremony of immersing the deceascd body of a monk in a river or the ocean.

Kali: the Divine Mother, representing the timeless aspect of Divinity.

karma sannyasa: to renounce attachment while performing any action - to remain calmly in the fontanel and compassionately detached while doing any kind of work and perceiving that the Soul is the real doer in your body.

Katha Upanishad: one of the principal Upanishads within the Vedic tradition.

khechari: a special mudra practiced in Yoga. It is derived from *kha* ('space') and *char* ('to roam') - to roam in the vacuum of meditation.

Kriya Yoga, Kriya: the science of self-control and self-realization through meditation.

kulaguru: the word is composed of *kula* and *guru*. *Kula* means dynasty or family. *Kulaguru* is the tradition of dynastical Guru-lineage where the son of the *kulaguru* carries out the responsibility of the Guru, after the death of his father.

Kumbha Mela: is a religious congregation in the Hindu tradition celebrated in four different places, Hardwar, Allahabad, Ujjain and Nasik, at three years intervals. The faithful gather to have a holy bath in the river and discuss different aspects of spirituality.

kundalini: the untapped spiritual energy remaining in each human being.

laddu: Indian sweet.

mahasamadhi: the final conscious exit of a realized person from the body.

mantra: sacred formula, different prayers in Sanskrit.

matrika nyasa: placing the fifty letters of the Sanskrit alphabet (*matrikas*) in the whole body; to experience calmness and divinity throughout the whole body.

maya: literally 'she who measures', the cosmic delusive force.

moha: delusion, dejection and infatuation.

mukti: liberation or freedom.

navakalevara: a special celebration at the Jagannath Temple, Puri.

niranjanastaka stotra: a collection of prayers in eight stanzas, usually chanted by the monks before meditation.

nirvikalpa samadhi: the highest state of cosmic consciousness, a formless state in which there is no distinction between subject and object, oneness with *Brahman*.

Oriya: an Indian language spoken in the state of Orissa.

paramahamsa: 'supreme swan'. The swan is the only creature that is capablc of separating milk from water once they have been mixed together. Similarly, a *paramahamsa* is the realized Master who, having attained the supreme yogic state, or *nirvikalpa samadhi*, can always distinguish between the real (*sa*) and the unreal (*ham*).

paramartha: supreme attainment; spiritual treasure.

paramukti: the supreme state of liberation.

Patanjali: a sage and the author of the Yoga Sutras, a classical text on Yoga.

patravali: compilation of letters.

pranams: to surrender or to bow down.

prasad: 'grace, clarity or tranquility', that which comes from God as His grace, gift and greetings; consecrated food.

prema: love for God.

pundita: man of knowledge, a priest and a scholar of Sanskrit.

purnahuti: a final oblation offered in a Vedic fire ceremony.

purushottama: the Supreme almighty Father or the supreme Self.

rudraksha: the seed of a special tree, which is used to make the rosary used by monks and Yogis.

sadhaka: a meditator, who trades the path of spirituality.

Sadhana Samara: literally the battle of spiritual practice, a book with commentary on *Durga*

sahasradala padma: also known as *sahasrara*, is the thousand petal lotus on the crown of the head, considered as the place of concentration and emancipation.

samadhi: unity with the Almighty Father; merged and engrossed in God-consciousness; complete freedom from nature's three *gunas*; the eighth and last limb of *Patanjali's ashtanga yoga* system.

samadhi mandira: *samadhi* here means the burial place of a monk. *Mandira* means temple. It is a temple constructed on the tomb of a realized Master. A place of prayer and meditation as well as a sanctuary.

sandesh: Indian sweet.

sannyasa: renunciation; *sannyasa* is not merely a renunciation of the physical world, it is inner detachment.

Saraswati Puja: the worship of *Saraswati*, godess of knowledge, speech and music. This festval is usually in the month of January and February.

satsanga: 'association with the real', good company; spiritual communion; to be established in the Self.

satsanga sabha: a congregation to discuss spiritual topics.

shambavi: a yogic practice of meditation with the eyes open to perceive light.

Shaptasati or *Chandi*: written by Brahmarshi Satyadev.

snanapurnima: the full moon in the month of June, dedicated to Lord *Jagannath* as the day of a ritual bath.

Subhadra: the presiding godess among three principal deities in Jagannath Temple. Sister of Krishna who married Arjuna in the Mahabharata.

swami: the master, the husband, the owner and also used before the name of a monk.

vairagya: non-attachment or dispassion.

vaishvanara agni: the fire in the lumbar center.

vilva: wood apple, a holy tree for the Hindus. It's leaves are offered in the worship of Shiva, Durga and Kali etc. The leaves and fruits have a high medicinal value in Ayurveda.

vishvaguru: universal Guru, world teacher.

yajna: a special fire ceremony conducted according to the Vedic rites, where oblation of ghee and other materials are offered in the holy fire, with the chanting of *mantras*.

yogacharya: teacher of Yoga.

yoganidra: *yoga* means oneness of body and Soul, and *nidra* means sleep; it is constant awareness of the inner Self or conscious *samadhi*.

Names

Anneliese Ma: a long time disciple of Baba who works as the secretary of the Vienna Ashram.

Arun Chatterjee: a college friend of Triloki, in whose room he first saw Gurudev's photo.

Bimal Ghosh: a disciple of Baba in Calcutta.

Bishwanath Baba: a centenarian monk from Orissa, belonging to the Alekh Samprada order, who left his body about a decade ago, author of many spiritual books.

Brahmanandaji: a long time disciple of Baba and a friend and companion of Triloki during their Ashram life, his pre-monastic name was Satyendra Nath Ray.

Brahmarshi Satyadev: a renowned spiritual Master, brother disciple of Gurudev, and author of many spiritual books in Bengali.

Brigitte Ma: pre-monastic name of Swami Mangalananda Giri, a long-time disciple of Gurudev in the Vienna Ashram.

Christine Ma: a *yogacharya* of Gurudev and devoted disciple who has helped Gurudev's work in many ways.

Don Baba: a *yogacharya* of Gurudev, center leader of New York.

Debi Baba: Debi Prasad Chatterjee, nephew of Gurudev and his first disciple, a *yogacharya*; practicing attorney in Calcutta.

Dharanidhara Pakhira: a householder disciple of Shriyukteshwar, who often visited the Karar Ashram. He left his body a few years ago.

Dr. Adwaita Mohanty: Professor and Head of the Department of Economics at Utkal University, Bhubaneshwar. Teacher and Research Supervisor of Triloki for his Ph.D. in Economics.

Dr. Harinath Bathina: a long-time disciple of Baba. Scientist working in the USA.

Dr. Narottam Gaan: a long time disciple of Gurudev, who teaches Political Science in Orissa, who knew Triloki as a student.

Dr. Niranjan Pradhan: a long time disciple of Gurudev, in whose residence Prajnanananda/Triloki received the first *darshan* of Gurudev.

Dr. Ojha Baba: Dr. H.K. Ojha, a long time disciple of Gurudev in Calcutta, a practicing Homeopath.

Dr. Peter Bäurle: a long time disciple of Gurudev and a Psychiatrist, whose house in Beheimgasse, Vienna, was the first Ashram in Austria.

Dr. S.N.Battacharya: Gurudevs third eldest brother, a medical doctor, later on initiated into Kriya Yoga by Gurudev; passed away three years ago.

Gerd Baba: long time disciple of Gurudev in Vienna.

Jay Narayan Mishra: *yogacharya* and a long-time disciple of Gurudev.

Justice Lingaraj Rath: a long time disciple of Gurudev, who offered his hospitality to Gurudev on many occasions.

Jutta Ma: a disciple of Gurudev and sister of Brigitte Ma.

Mahatma Gandhi: the father of the Indian Freedom Movement, a humanitarian, philanthropist who practiced *ahimsa* or non-violence, in public as well as in his personal life.

Manoranjan: Triloki's friend from school and University, who was initiated into Kriya on the same day.

Mrs. Manorama Mahapatra: ex-professor of Economics, and teacher of Triloki. Later on became the editor of the 'The Samaj', a leading daily newspaper in Orissa.

Meera, Meera Bai: a poet, saint and a mystique of 15th Century India, whose extreme love for God made many miracles.

Peter Baba: Rajarshi Peter van Breukelen, a *yogacharya* of Gurudev, who teaches Kriya Yoga in Europe and runs the Ashram in Holland.

Radhanath Rath: a renowned physician, retired Director of Health, Government of Orissa, Gurudev's long-time disciple.

Raghabananda Nayak: *yogacharya* and a long-time disciple of Gurudev.

Ramachandra Hota: pre-monastic name of Swami Shuddhananda Giri, friend and companion of Triloki from his school days.

Ramakrishna Paramahamsa: a great saint of India, in the 19th Century, who brought a spiritual renaissance to India and abroad through his worthy disciples like Swami Vivekananda, Swami Abhedananda etc.

Ray Baba: pre-monastic name of Swami Brahmananda Giri.

Roland Baba: a long time disciple of Gurudev from Germany.

Sankaracharya of Kanchi Kamakoti Peetha: one of the *sankaracharya's* of India, spiritual heads of Hinduism.

Satya Baba: a disciple of Gurudev in Calcutta.

Shrimanta Baba: a *brahmachari* staying in the Cuttack Ashram.

Shuddhananda: literally the bliss of purity.

Sitanath Patnaik: an engineer, a long time disciple of Gurudev, who was present during Triloki's initiation.

Sujogya: a collage friend of Triloki

Swami Nigamananda: his pre-monastic name was Nalinikanta Bhattacharya, a renowned and highly realized Yogi in the early part of the Twentieth Century.

Swami Sivananda: founder of the Divine Life Society in Rishikesh. A renowned spiritual Master of India.

Swami Swarupananda: a reputed monk in India, author of many books. A source of inspiration in young Triloki to lead a spiritual life.

Swami Vivekananda: disciple of Ramakrishna Paramahamsa, who delivered talks in the Parliament of World's Religions in Chicago in the year 1863. A great sage.

Triloki Dash: pre-monastic name of Swami Prajnanananda Giri.

Ulrich Baba: long time disciple of Gurudev from Germany.

Vijay Krishna: Paramahamsa Hariharananda's first Guru and a renowned *jnana yogi*.

Wolf Baba: a disciple in Hamburg.

Names of Places and Rivers

Ananda Bazaar: the market of bliss, a place inside the Jagannath Temple, where people get *mahaprasad* or the holy food from the Temple.

Assam: a hilly state in the North East part of India.

Balighai: a place in the outskirts of Puri, located on the way to the Sun Temple of Konnark, where Hariharananda Gurukulam is established.

Bengal: a state in the East coast of India.

Bhawanipatna: a town in Western Orissa.

Bhubaneshwar: the capital city of Orissa.

Calcutta: the capital city of Bengal.

Chicago: prominent city in the USA, where the Parliament of World's Religions was held in 1893.

Cuttack: a historical city over a thousand years old. The cultural center of Orissa, where Triloki completed his University education, taught Economics and founded an Ashram.

Ganga: a holy river in India, on whose banks numerous holy places are located. It originates from the glacier of Gomukh and merges in the ocean at Gangasagar.

Hardwar: a holy city of the Hindus in North India, where the river *Ganga* enters the plane, leaving the mountain path.

Himalayas: the mountains located in the North of India, believed as a place of great spiritual significance

	and from which many rivers have originated. Literally the place of coolness.
Jagannath Temple:	located in the city of Puri, where Lord Jagannath, the Lord of the Universe, is worshipped by the Hindus over thousands of years.
Jagatpur:	located on the bank of the river *Mahanadi*, in the state of Orissa, where Prajnana Mission has its headquarters.
Jharsuguda:	a town in Western Orissa.
Karar Ashram:	founded by Shriyukteshwarji in the year 1903, in the holy city of Puri, on the East Coast of India.
Mahanadi:	the longest river of Orissa.
Orissa:	a state in the East coast of India.
Pattamundai:	Birthplace of Swami Prajnanananda, about 60 miles from Cuttack.
Puri:	a holy city for the Hindus, one of the four most significant places of pilgrimage in India.
Ravenshaw College:	located in Cuttack, a well-known educational institution of Orissa, where Triloki studied and later on taught Economics.
Rishikesh:	a holy city on the foothills of the Himalayas and the bank of the *Ganga*.
Rourkela:	an industrial city in Western Orissa, where Triloki began his teaching career.
Sambalpur:	a city in the West of Orissa.
St. Gallen:	a city in Switzerland.

Vienna: capital city of Austria, where Gurudev started an Ashram and Triloki Dash came in 1994 to carry out Gurudev's work.

Yamuna: a holy river in North India, originating in the Himalayas and merging in the *Ganga* at Allahabad.

About the Author

Paramahamsa Prajnanananda, the disciple and the designated successor of Paramahamsa Hariharananda, has taken on the mission of bringing the ancient secret teachings within the reach of common people who are thirsting for spiritual knowledge. Paramahamsa Prajnanananda was born in 1960 in the village of Pattamundai in Orissa, India. He has always been a sincere seeker of truth. After a childhood filled with prayer and a youth enriched by education joined with meditation, the former Triloki Dash became a caring teacher as a professor of Economics and guided and inspired many of his students spiritually.

As a college student, through an unquenchable thirst for God, he met many saints and visited many Ashrams in the Himalayas, looking for a spiritual guide. While still a student, he met his Master Paramahamsa Hariharananda, who initiated him into the path of Kriya Yoga. Brahmachari Triloki Dash was later initiated into the glorious path of *Sannyas* by his Master, becoming Swami Prajnanananda Giri. On August 10, 1998, on his 39th birthday, the title of Paramahamsa, the highest title reserved for monks, who attain the summit of realization, who are inspired and divine teachers, guides and saints, was conferred upon him by his loving and divine Master Paramahamsa Hariharananda.

A truly powerful and extremely loving teacher, author and speaker on world religion, well versed in the scriptures of the East and West, he combines a divine compassion for humanity with his love for God and his mastery of complex philosophical thoughts. His vast knowledge and his oratory and intellectual skills are fully utilized in interpreting deep philosophical thoughts in the light of modern science and psychology. His metaphorical interpretation of the scriptures is very unique. Using Kriya Yoga as a reference point and an interpretative tool, Prajnananandaji manages to reveal the hidden truths contained in the most complex passages of the sacred texts in ways, which make the meanings relevant and helpful in our daily lives.

With thought-provoking statements and revelatory explanations, quotations from the Bible and the Bhagavad Gita, and incidents from the lives of great Souls, Paramahamsa Prajnanananda distils the wisdom of the ages into clear, relevant instructions on leading a moral and spiritual life in the world today. Without being overly pedantic, yet incorporating the texts of countless scriptures within his lectures, Paramahamsa Prajnanandaji does what most religious teachers stop short of doing and what most of us are thirsting for: he gives step by step methods for achieving self-realization. Gearing his lectures to the modern world of East and West, peppering them with colorful anecdotes, in his humorous yet compassionate style, with constant words of encouragement to those who must continue to live in the world, he guides disciples with the love of a mother. To those who are baffled by the vastness of ancient scriptural wisdom, the clear, concise and immensely helpful hints and guidance he provides, helps to make sense of book learning.

The power of his teachings lies in their simplicity and direct relevance to our lives. He teaches one of the simplest truths of the scriptures. One needs not only the desire for salvation, but also the guidance of the Guru and the regular practice of meditation and then and only then comes realization.

Paramahamsa Prajnanananda teaches only one lesson: the lesson of love. Through not only the study of the scriptures, and the practice of meditation, but through every action and every breath, he urges us to realize that we are all divine and to achieve that blissful state of divine love and contentment, through basic self-discipline and the practice of simple yogic principles.

His loving guidance and deep compassion have won him the devotion and faith of countless disciples around the world whose lives he has transformed.

Other Available Books

The Path of Love

by Paramahamsa Prajnanananda

Through basic self-discipline and the practice of simple yogic principles, in every action and in every breath, Paramahamsa Prajnanananda leads us on the ascending path to attain the purest form of love.

Published in 2001 ISBN 3-902038-07-1

Life and Values

by Paramahamsa Prajnanananda

Presents the way to understand and to master the art of living, inculcating the values in it and thereby to make our life purposeful and beautiful.

Published in 2001 ISBN 3-902038-09-8

Akṣara Tattva - Sacred Syllables

by Paramahamsa Prajnanananda

This small volume gives us a metaphorical and mythological introduction to the inner principles of the Sanskrit alphabet, giving deep insight to the scientific language itself and its spiritual heritage.

Published in 2001 ISBN 81-87825-02-2

Divine Blossoms

by Paramahamsa Prajnanananda

A much needed handbook on the Lives and Teachings of the sacred lineage of Kriya Masters until today.

Published in 2000 ISBN 3-902038-04-7

Discourses on the Bhagavad Gita—Book Two

by Paramahamsa Prajnanananda

An interpretation of the Gita as a yogic path through karma (action), jnana (knowledge) and bhakti (devotion), in the light of Kriya Yoga.

Published in 2000 ISBN 3-901665-26-9

THE UNIVERSE WITHIN

by Paramahamsa Prajnanananda

A fascinating analogy between the outer universe and the human body. Through intimate knowledge of our chakras we can tap the source of everlasting happiness.

Printed in 2000 ISBN 3-902038-03-9

NAVA DURGA, THE MULTIPLE FORM OF THE MOTHER

by Paramahamsa Prajnanananda

Takes Mother Durga as the source of inspiration and a symbol of man's spiritual advancement.

Published in 2000 ISBN 3-90166528-5

THE BHAGAVAD GITA IN THE LIGHT OF KRIYA YOGA—BOOK ONE

by Paramahamsa Hariharananda, compiled by Paramahamsa Prajnanananda

This first part of three volumes has an in-depth analysis of Karma Yoga or the path of action, and the practical benefits of meditation.

First Published in 1996, Second Edition in 2000 ISBN 0-9639107-1-X

THE BHAGAVAD GITA IN THE LIGHT OF KRIYA YOGA—BOOK TWO

by Paramahamsa Hariharananda, compiled by Paramahamsa Prajnanananda

The second part of three volumes, this book concentrates on the path of self-unfoldment that leads towards spiritual knowledge and divine love.

Published in 1998 ISBN 0-9639107-1-X

THE BHAGAVAD GITA IN THE LIGHT OF KRIYA YOGA—BOOK THREE

by Paramahamsa Hariharananda, compiled by Paramahamsa Prajnanananda

The third and last volume dwells on how to get rid of our demonic qualities and develop our divine nature and describes what type of life we should lead, what type of food we should eat and what work we must perform. It takes the individual towards the ultimate goal of human existence; to reach unity with God and find liberation.

Published in 1999 ISBN 0-9639107-2-8

Kriya Yoga: The Scientific Process of Soul Culture and Essence of All Religions

by Paramahamsa Hariharananda

A quintessential glimpse into a great Yogi's philosophy as well as a practical guide to self-realization. First Edition in 1977

5th Revised Edition in 1998 ISBN 81-86713-05-0

Paramahamsa Hariharananda: River of Compassion

by Paramahamsa Prajnanananda

This biography, written by his loving disciple and designated successor, contains a wealth of details about the Life and Teaching of this great enlightened Master, including many touching testimonials of those whose lives Paramahamsa Hariharananda has transformed.

Published in 1999 ISBN 3-901665 24-2

Mahavatar Babaji: The Eternal Light of God

by Swami Prajnanananda Giri

This charming little book contains the essence of the sacred Teachings of this greatest and the most mysterious of all realized Masters.

Published in 1997 ISBN 81-86713-06-9

Lahiri Mahasaya: Fountainhead of Kriya Yoga

by Paramahamsa Prajnanananda

This biography contains the divine message of Lahiri Mahasaya, the beloved and chosen disciple of Babaji. It describes how this great Yogi carried out his mission of spreading the science of Kriya Yoga, while leading the ordinary life of a householder and eventually attaining God-realization.

Published in 1999 ISBN 3-901665-22- 6

Swami Shriyukteshwar: Incarnation of Wisdom

by Paramahamsa Prajnanananda

The Life and Teachings of a great Guru whose discipline and rigorous training shaped the lives of many prominent disciples, including Paramahamsa Yogananda and Paramahamsa Hariharananda.

Published in 1999 ISBN3-901665-23-4

Discourses on the Bhagavad Gita, Book One

by Paramahamsa Prajnanananda

Using Kriya Yoga as a reference point and an interpretative tool, this advanced Yogi manages to reveal the hidden truths contained in the most complex passages of this sacred text.

First Printed in 1998

Second Revised Edition 1999 ISBN 3-901665-25-0

Yoga: Pathway to the Divine

by Paramahamsa Prajnanananda

Paramahamsa Prajnanananda gives a step-by-step method in order to attain spiritual progress in our daily lives.

Published in 1999 ISBN 3-901665-21-8

The Torah, The Bible and Kriya Yoga: Metaphorical Explanation of the Torah and the New Testament, in the Light of Kriya Yoga

by Paramahamsa Prajnanananda

This work dwells on the common essence and universal truths that lie hidden beneath these sacred texts, and includes their interpretation in the light of Kriya Yoga.

Published in 1996 ISBN 81-86713-00-X

Words of Wisdom: Stories and Parables of Paramahamsa Hariharananda
compiled by Swami Prajnanananda Giri
A helpful record of the wisdom contained in the words of a realized Master, which reveals a high element of spiritual truth that can be translated as a practical guide for everyday life.
Published in 1996 ISBN 3-901665-00-5

Nectar Drops: Sayings of Paramahamsa Hariharananda
compiled by Swami Prajnanananda Giri
This small volume captures the most representative sayings and practical everyday advice from this great living realized Master.
Published in 1996 ISBN 3-9011665-01-3

To be released soon:

Jnana Shankalini Tantra in the Light of Kriya Yoga
by Paramahamsa Prajnanananda
A long awaited and most interesting examination of the often misinterpreted ancient tantric texts revealing subtle truths hidden beneath the texts.

Yoga Sutra of Patanjali
by Paramahamsa Prajnanananda
Systematic written exposition and metaphorical explanation of the Yoga Sutra with commentaries by the great Yogi, Lahiri Mahasaya.

Kriya Yoga Contacts

For more information and/or copies of other books please contact the following centers:

USA

Mother Centre USA
Kriya Yoga Institute
P.O. Box 924615
Homestead, FL 33092-4615
Tel: + 305-247 1960
Fax: + 305-248 1951
institute@kriya.org
www.kriya.org

INDIA

Prajnana Mission
Kriya Yoga Ashram
Nimpur, P.O. Jagatpur
Cuttack 754021, Orissa
Tel: + 91 671 682724
Fax: + 91 671 682887
ssgiri@cal3.vsnl.net.in
www.prajnanamission.org

EUROPE

Mother Centre Europe
Kriya Yoga Centre Vienna
Pottendorferstrasse 69
A-2523 Tattendorf
Austria
Tel: + 1 43 2253 81 491
Fax: + 1 43 2253 80 462
kriya.yoga.centre@aon.at
www.kriyayoga-europe.org

Kriya Yoga Centrum
Heezerweg 7
NL-6029-PP, Sterksel
The Netherlands
Tel: + 31 40-2265576
Fax: + 31 40-2265612
kriya.yoga@worldonline.nl